GROUND RULES

Ground Rules:

THE BEST OF THE SECOND DECADE OF ABOVE/GROUND PRESS 2003–2013

EDITED BY ROB MCLENNAN
WITH AN INTRODUCTION BY GIL MCELROY

TABLE OF CONTENTS

INTRODUCTION: AN INTEGRAL

GIL MCELROY

Another measure, another decade, another ten. One twice over, now.

Ping.

Working out of Ottawa, poet and publisher rob mclennan's baby, above/ground press, marks a second decade of the production of broadsheets, chapbooks, magazines, and anthologies that trace out the best shapes of the best of contemporary Canadian (and, increasingly, international) poetry. From the span of that second ten of years, he has compiled this book of traceries: a selection of work by writers ranging from the likes of the late bpNichol, Artie Gold, and Robert Kroetsch, to the living derek beaulieu, Rachel Zolf, Eric Folsom, Natalie Simpson, etc., all collected here as representative of a decade's aesthetic count.

Pong.

So *Best of the Second Decade* itself traces out the traceries, contextualizing the range of poetries contained herein. This is, of course, a form of meta-mark-making happening: the creation, at the level of the press itself, of an overarching, curatorially established figure or shape that, when examined closely at what could be likened to an "atomic" or "cellular" level of an individual text itself, is made up of the poetries of those poets mclennan has championed (and, in the interests of full disclosure, I'm fortunate enough to be one of those poets and some of those poetries). It's a figure or shape – an aesthetic container, if you will – the absolute limits of which can be metaphorically described in two rather different ways.

Ping.

The former would involve the early computer game of Pong. I'm old enough to have played this when it was new back in the 1970s on old black & white televisions. If you're not familiar with it, it comprised a moving dot of light that was the ball, and an em dash of white that would be the paddle which could be moved vertically up and down one side of the screen by the player to hit the bit of light that would appear to be bouncing off the internal edges of the tv screen. The better you got at the game, the faster the light moved. To stretch a metaphor to the breaking point, like some self-contained modernist poem Pong comprised a self-contained system based on a simple set of coded rules, one into which a degree of new information could be inserted affecting one variable (the speed at which the game occurred).

Pong.

The other metaphor involves the late American poet, Louis Zukofsky. I'm not comparing his work to an obsolete computer game, nor even trying to contextually frame it so as to articulate an elaborate "either/or" set of contrasting oppositions, but rather invoking a "cellular" level bit of text from his magnum opus, "A":

About my *poetics* —

$$\int_{speech}^{music}$$

An integral
Lower limit speech
Upper limit music

Ping. Pong.

We typically only instance the latter two lines when referencing this best-known of Zukofsky's quotes from "A-12", usually forgoing the critically important and overarching mention of "An integral." It's a mathematical reference, a mathematical sign (from calculus, actually), a mathematical symbol that Zukofsky pertinently situates between the isolated nouns "music" and "speech" and which refers, not surprisingly, to the relationship between the two, and the rich, fecund area of possible poetics that comprises the space that separates them.

Higher. Ping.

Lower. *Pong.*

Zukofsky here articulates the reach of his poetics, denoting the incorporation of the common rhythms and textures of everyday speech (as he would have encountered them in period New York City) and the "higher" sophistication of music (which is actually formally incorporated into "A" later on beginning with "A-24" and continuing to the end of the work). The integral sign signifies relationship, and while we might think of common speech and music as oppositional extremes, one perhaps aesthetically superior to the other, Zukofsky's use of the symbol tells us that neither is to be priorized over the other, that the imperative of an equivalency of relationship reigns.

Lower limit, then, *Pong*. Upper limit Zukofsky.

Ping.

In a semantic field curatorially circumscribed by such relational metaphors, the poetries of *Best of the Second Decade* occur, unpredictably ricocheting back and forth between the boundaries, never spiraling entirely out of semantic range into the sheer, mathematical abstraction of pure music (though most certainly touching upon it, incorporating its sonic elements and effects, referencing its possibilities, embracing its sensations), but also never falling and being swallowed up the chasms of the basest forms of textbook, instruction-manual speech that cleaves as closely as possible to a narrow, rigid 1:1 correspondence between a thing and its sign (though most certainly touching upon them, incorporating their sonic elements and effect, referencing their possibilities, embracing their sensations).

above/ground press and the work included in *Best of the Second Decade* traverse the territorial whole of the poetic integral Zukofsky announced and embraced, articulating some of the myriad forms of a world that might exist between the limits of Pong and music.

To paraphrase the words of ancient mapmakers who had reached to the edges of the knowable world and could map no further, and so fell back on their imaginings of the wonders that lay beyond: here be many dragons.

Ping.

March 2013

INDIVIDUAL POEMS

DOUBLET

Artie Gold

I rode her a different direction
like a constant collision lodged

ROTATOR CUFF AT 33 1/3

Mark Cochrane

Body is a made thing, time-share, a Christ
or T.S. Garp. At 33

a guy glistens
like rocks on the seashore, peaks out, surfs.
Then, biblically, thingness: a rust bucket
you cannot trade.

Rotator cuff: military press.
Round round
get around. Problem is a noun
can be adjective, it verbs you, not
even this buzz cut
prevents a tearing

of tendons & sheaths. Push-pull
chest regimen
wrecked & ho
hum—entropy. *Smile*, throw it away, it's perfect

said Brian Wilson.
Beached jogger, advised to rest
his swollen feet. Tongues pop
from the Nikes, saying
Shut up / already
damn: oracle

e.g. husband
to the wingèd goddess. Fatigued
like any fan belt
or vinyl on long play. Never again

to rev like a single.

SUIT

Suzanne Zelazo

This is the overload. Permutational meditation on becoming more unlike oneself. Undoubt in the lounge where intrigue meets mending. A prefix generation against slow grain repair. I've seen the best minds of my generation bolt in violation, a sampling. We are an accompaniment. Total saturation and current meant for mining. Quake the tone, a tome for allusion, once the syntax of infrequency.

A vessel noun among us. Until now, a shade. A leaf clad in service. Empirical definition of shift in syntax, or an antique coffer central to the sight passage. Pause and start again. Blast the discourse, form a reprint, San Marino California, crisp against unmoving pardon. We were all Others overridden by an ending. Unlace the dogma in stanzas. Un-Cagein, too much refuse is an address.

Smooth sonneteer gave me the implication of verse, its formulation of likeness. A season of improper sound and harmony. In the nets maybe, overriding the portion of extract. Two no less incidental press the rhythm, barbell simulation. Much less a service than a structure of accord. In gratitude, if case to undulate. Import the idiom we historicize and mitigate. Centre count the talisman. Nightchant burrowed in steel-rim tradition.

A phoneme plots possibility, proof-sheets of compulsion and fluid repetition. It can save you. Acronym assemblage, much like composition, each one's Athenian. Luna less unnumbered and housepressed. Records of the inside out. Who is whose left for owning, leasing solitary company. I thought the visual was mythologic, including pessimism, but its left, looking for certainty of audience and I pile more syntax in the leading. Don't forget the gathering.

Three and six's a conviction. Isometric origin. Undivide the division becoming whole.

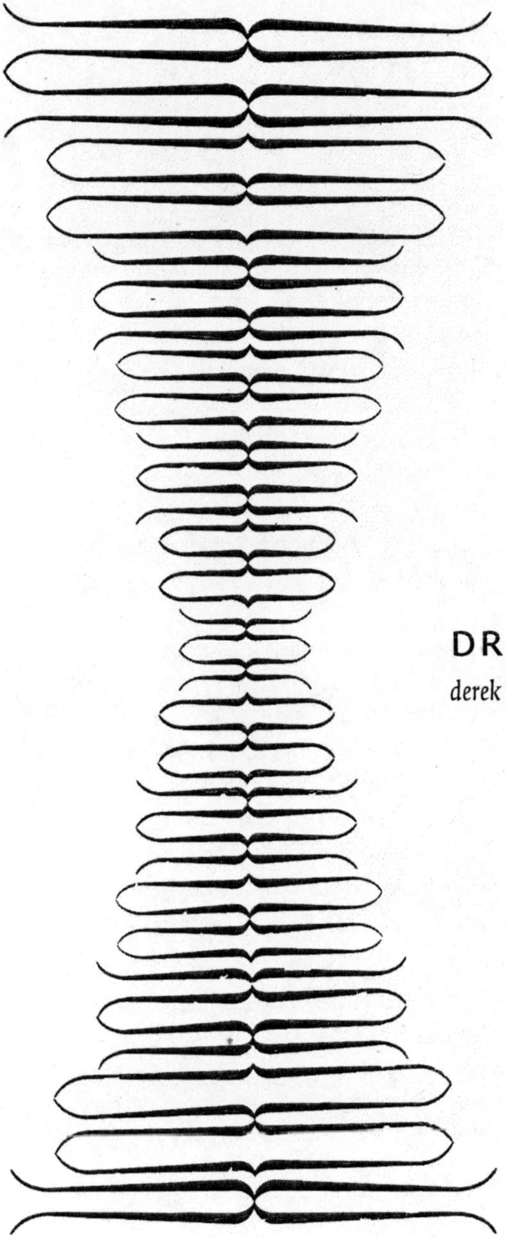

DREAM POEM FOR DIETER ROTH #1

derek beaulieu

UNTITLED #3

derek beaulieu

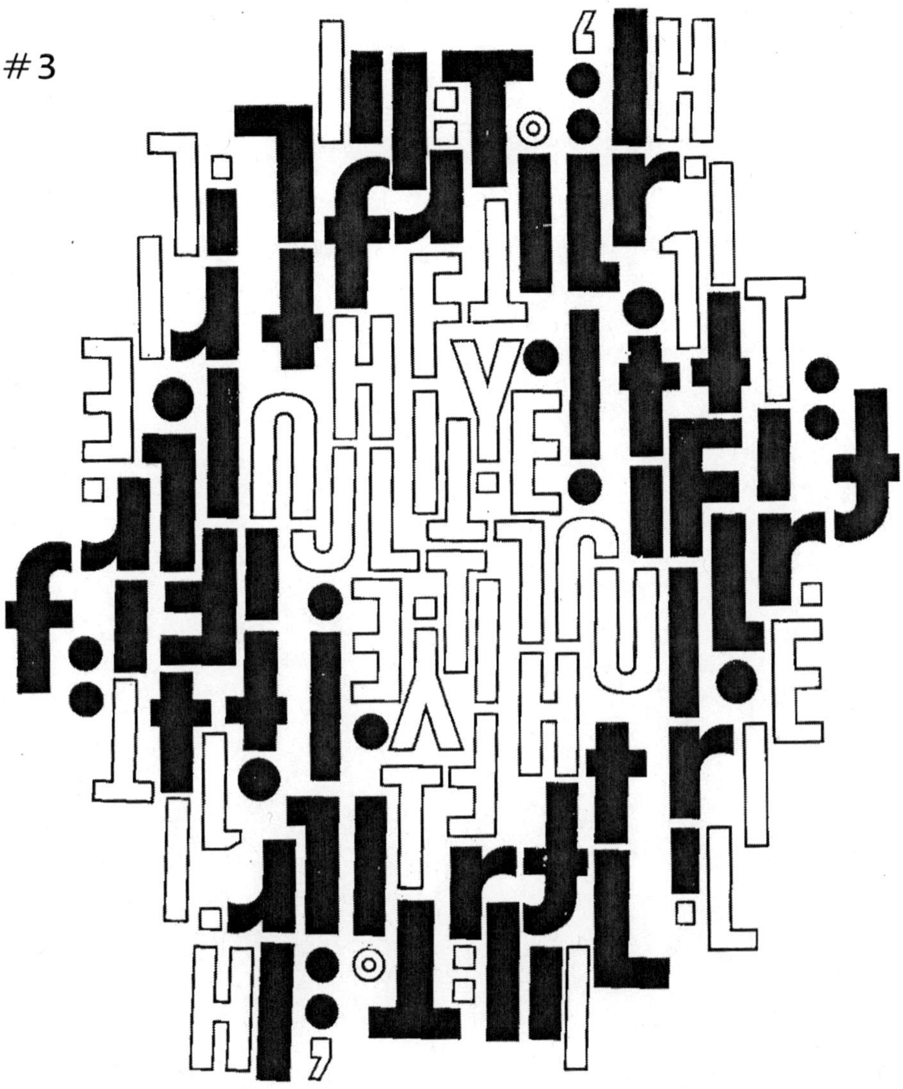

NIGHT ZOO

Stephanie Bolster

Dogs ravaged the yard where yesterday
rabbits and toads. The dead
fed to the cages and the dark.
The mouth of the mouth.

Plants dangled from pegs
beside padlocks. Reaching,
though they weren't.

A dark stain on concrete.
A little water.

Let's go, I said,
meaning stay.

IVRE

Amanda Earl

weaves
clochard de la rue
/ vagrant
pavement straggler
drunk is bitten, then gulped
lc lived with buddhist monks
bottles of wine a day
out of control
yet still in
bateau for water
boaters
pushed through / beer hop
glide through

how dizzy
you make

CHAPBOOKS

WHAT EXILE THIS

Nathanaël

(first published, January 2002)

Written in October 2001, *What Exile This* belongs to a period of effervescent activity and significant transformation in the corpus of Nathanaël's work, coincident with the writing of what would be *Je Nathanaël*, a text with no mother tongue, and no original version to speak of. It is arguable that this intense period of writing, carried out in Guelph, set in motion the various departures that would impel Nathanaël toward Chicago, and severance not only from prior nominal locations, but elements, also, of her œuvre, which she has since disavowed.

Feign – Bastard! The copulant word.

(There is cock in it
disheartened perhaps and oddly distended
from here the eye grabs hold of it
pulls upon it for sense or
queerly the ghettoed smile arouses
distrust What did you expect?

There is cock in it to be sure
or some such thing moistening the intrepid
thigh though in hindsight what was or could
have been hard is an optical illusion
This (*Ceci*) was a book to be written but
the words have been blackened out and the bodies
thrown into the river (rejected, mind

Translated thusly: cabrón or mamzerim for we are many.

The Iberian context offers up its multiplicity.
Did I say betwixt? It was a word to my sister.
The continents are shifting and I misplaced my city.

A Quick Lesson in Geography

Mores   a door in a hill   ritually speaking

dusk

There was no door to speak for
no door to knock upon   I came for you

lighting candles.

Context: What Paré calls *Shifting* the acultural
text linguistically, grammatically
adept but lacking in content

Who you were before words never mind tongue
there'll be time enough for that

But what will you say?

Take any trajectory but for the sake of concision this one because it is familiar to me (although not the places themselves, I have not been). Still. Or any other. *Nabebess* – Je prends ton mal.

You never leave it behind.

P.S. A word is so a trajectory.

So to the *Shifting* body. Le *Shifting* really but for ease of

Albion Hotel : Men's washroom.
Hand tucked into your pants, you adjust your cock, balls nestled comfortably against your clit. In the mirror you check for stubble. Later some guy buys you a beer : Stephen, let me buy you a beer.

Bookshelf : Men's washroom.
Jon's at the urinal taking a piss, you're on the shitter. He can't go. Hand tucked into your pants, you adjust your cock, balls nestled comfortably against your clit. Someone wants to know what you're wearing. You read a poem instead.

Jimmy Jazz : Men's washroom.
You don't go.

Everywhere I'm a faggot. Still, no one gets it.

What did you expect? Grammar is its own fundamentalism.

Note to Stephen : Next time pack a hard-on.

But Stephen *la bâtardise*

the river threw you up and your sharp little blade.

Note to F. : Spilling he is spilling himself
and the consequences on his body are many
not just the cries of a student (such a
wretched noise) every country contains lost
languages why not this one? Should we not
be *Shifting* out of ourselves away from our tongues?
Stephen himself is quite lost. He wants a word
for it. What will you tell him? What word will
you give him. He is quite lost now

You spoke out in favour of migrations saying the body is migratory *ça va de soi* but you never went anywhere. You insisted on what you called physical nomadism wrapping

Noise the body's ventriloquism or

What wars   the body moves in keeping with the contextual strain

When leaving a place   keep
(*Fratres*   &tc

What exile this

When Stephen said gender someone said So who's the lucky
girl. It was his accent. He never said *gendre* (and what a
stretch anyway!) but it was too late. The town hall was
booked for the wedding. He tucked his hand into his pants
and stroked his cock enjoying the twitch of his clit.
Nothing ever came of it.

What shift?

Le corps illegibly

Dear Stephen madness will come. You will
walk in a place and stones will gather
in your shoes. You will return there often
because of the river and the swollen sky.
Everything will change and you will
forgive yourself for wanting even that.

Touch everything twice.

In the poem the body drifts away from language.
The movement is termed dissident.
It is a sort of disloyalty and phrased in such a way
as to instill guilt.
Regardless of the absence of language, the concept
remains. You are guilt-ridden, even outside of speech.

You would walk naked if it weren't for words.
These are new migrations.
You are among the new defectors.
Stephen, there are hands wanting only to touch.
A letter burned white then red then black onto your skin.

L'armera. Guard it fiercely. Walk.

Several   or more   (merely) you are not in it for (mother) tongue.
Somewhere a bus moves along a dirt road. Ancestry is a solipsistic
ideal,

Someone places an order for kosher meat

détrompe-toi these fingers too are blooded
there's no adage for this   –

Stephen you too are accountable for

What lineage found body hard (yours)

& *Shifting*

echoes of that (intrisic) and others

P.S. Dear Stephen touch what moves you. Touch with the conviction of its existence and the certainty that it will elude you. There is no ritual for

demonstrably

You were saying

After

The ground falls away from your feet. You hesitate before tumbling into another body, another accent, another form. There is no refuge from tongue, no place small enough, intricate enough, to retreat to. You stop taking buses and trains. You leave your bicycle out in the rain. You are intrigued by the concept of rust, what the body does in heat. The sea floods a beach you've never been to, and you won't go now, not now that the beach is flooded and you have broken the line (of thought) from mother to daughter. What pulls countries apart.

Stephen, the streets of your city are strewn with chicken bones. There isn't a book you would read. Words break in your mouth. Your voice runs red into rivers.

THE MUSEUM OF PERCEPTION

Lisa Samuels

Text panel: Fortitude

In this panel a woman stands alert with her head
bent slightly to the right – she is listening to something,
the rain against the side of the house whose outside wall
shows – it is raining against the southern wall, a calendar
is pressed against the inner part, as though she could see
but it seems clear she is not actually looking. The room is
bare of everything except several hangings, and the woman,
and a square object whose use value is unclear. Outside
is more than rain – the sky has something in it ready to
announce itself, though we don't know what it might mean,
surrounding rain clouds, its shape uncertain and maybe
moving, we can't tell. The artist has named this piece
"Opacity," and I think I know why.

Text panel 33: "The City"

This photograph wrapped around a large cylinder demands the viewer encircle it with eyes that go ceaselessly in an effort to resolve the whole. Be careful of other visitors as you make this effort: some start from the left and some from the right of the room. These movements represent an inversion of the normal panorama. You are the outside world being observed by the figures wrapped around. It is not a tower despite its shape, which may be significant. As you look you will notice parts of it moving slightly. This is the artist having set up tiny thin windows of video stream that make one figure's eyes move toward you, then away, with one slight piece of sky shifting with change. There is no repetition in the action, because the cameras are recording from elsewhere. Try to imagine the other side of the artist's source material. Such suppressions are a normal part of seeing, the piece seems to say. You move narrowly and prove the point.

Text panel 17: Untitled

Here we have a balanced embarkation, as though the desert would seem to be a place that is not one and no one standing there. The sand undulates a wind made visible in it, a fine level blown continuously hovering just slightly above a surface one might call the ground. This portion of the piece is unresolved within an apparently static scene. However, the whole thing shears off from one angle, as though you step to the side and suddenly cannot see anything clearly. Step back again and see it is a balanced desert where no one is standing.

Text panel 21

In this moving sculpture we see happenstance grieving
for a better life. It doesn't appear any answer is available.
The guys are lurching toward each other, paleface wan
upwards, hands grappling, the sun nowhere in sight.
I think they are blind, these eyes. The surrounding buildings
are shown in reflection on the imperceptible shield that holds
the piece – they will turn toward you if you let them get too close.
That's why only one observer at a time is permitted into this room.
I stood here for half a day hoping to get the sight lined up
in revelatory fashion, but the figures never turned to me at all.

Text panel 49: "Citizenship"

In this painting a foreign woman ill-defined is waiting to go into a store, though she knows or doesn't that some danger is registered in her face. The outside world continuously wants her to do something other than what she is. That is the nature of observing. The front of the building has an indeterminate relation to her plans, as light arrives from the left side of the piece. The light is ideological and it hurts her. This is the sum of what's included, the lines streaked boldly across the taut-stretched canvas in directions we would normally expect.

Text panel 22: Activisme

In this piece the artist is accessing what will become Activisme,
the movement that atavistically inclined itself toward a sense of
wholistic community that somehow unified smaller portions of
attention than it is now apparently possible to activate. It is not serene.
Instead, the I wanders in a landscape full of parcels, seemingly
waiting for its purpose to become clear in regard to the boxes
and packaging that surround. It is a spare picture, somehow,
though every part of the canvas is full of some portion, color,
wave, shade, angle, or implied movement. The solitary I has its hand
on the side of one light oblong package and its face appears surprised.
It is as though the artist knew something was going to arrive
at any point, and only in a painting developed much later do
we see the connection: each of the parcels turns out to hold a human being
– babies, children, full-grown people held in fetal postures,
all waiting to emerge from those store-and-send devices that give this painting its name.

Text panel: Opposition

Half-way through the exhibit we now see a clue for it:
the trees outside are starving for a little forest to keep them dolorous company.
Having scrabbled through the corner of paintings
they discover their own cupidity to be seen is a wash of spite against their real existence.

They heave upwards their branching arms
and are flying out of the ground, their roots trailing
dirtily soughing off mounds and spits of dirt as they rise
heavily out of the surface mixed for them – their expressions are entirely a question
of movement and pull, naked undergirth exposed
in a painful refusal of participation in the two-dimensional scene.

It is difficult to see anything else in the painting.
It is almost as though you could imagine pulling
yourself out of this gallery, leaving your legs standing where they are
meshed in social ground and screaming as you are pulled lengthwise skyward.

Text panel: Wish

This piece is in the Irreal Movement: the kitten has turned
into a fish that was a baby and the plastic kept it safe inside
the box. Your hands are attached to the device by which
you animate this piece so as to see it. So your hands are
the instruments, clearly the artist wants you to think of
radiant particles if you go without gloves on.
This is symbolic of larger action: you may be thinking
this piece is too solitary, too unlike other parts of the gallery.
Because you stand here fondling and alone.
But everyone is putting their hands in you now.

Text panel 39: "possession=knowing"

In this piece we have a series of textual objects laid around the figure of a reclining female. She is wondering about which to pick up, we can see because her hands – blurred in representation – are moving over the objects in hesitation.

Or is it rapacity, spell-inducing, osmotic inclination, memory, tiredness, longing, or impossibility that motivates her hands?

Around her an imperfect sphere is shaped like an oval tethered to a square in turn surrounding her. The lines of these geometric enclosures are vague, not distinct. We think we see color throughout, and then we realize every contained thing appears in shades of grey. Only the outline of the containment lines, her body, and the edges of the textual objects are shimmering in muted lines of red, and green, and blue.

Text panel: Indigo

Several white shapes are surfacing in the arrows of the water
here, whose object existence is not clearly tethered to any
shore. It is a full blank surface, completely filled in, one
could scarcely tell it is water and not sky or darkness,
and then only because of the breaking aspect the
shapes create. That the surface can be penetrate
like that and leave off instances of splash,
mottled and relieved versions of shed
water. Whether it changes is also
hard to tell, because to see it
one must bend over the
cylindrical viewing
area foreshortened
by the artist
into a conical
tube, over which
we look for as long
as our place in line and
arching backs allow.

Text panel 50: Stasis

How to write about this piece? It is so moving, so unhabituated by the operative eye, it seems to quell anxiety by itself. I wish I had never seen it or that I could watch it all the time. The reality seems pictured by a sentience so obscure no satisfaction could touch it.

Starting from the lower left, it spreads out slowly in a dominant field oppressed by the followingness proceeding. The center is in a race with itself akin to the image on the other side of this very wall you might remember. I am antipathetic to the similarity. In the middle right side is a dormant figurine that seems to have no relation to its opposite. Or tenable. That is, the seen seems to know nothing about its correlation.

You see how bad I am with this. It seems the museum cannot trust me to tell you how to perceive more effectively. But spend some time in the upper right corner: the answer to leaving the scene seems braided in the fabric there, as though inserting your fingers into the patches will lead to sewing up the clothing this piece wants you to put on, even if temporarily, even if the "random scenic" of the catalog is only there to touch in a wired fashion, like what you put on in the morning to find yourself cupped and cloaked in the most ambitious way.

THE NAKED & THE NUDE

Rachel Zolf

❖

you enter the room

the room

sheds leaves

(,)

(,)

(,)

❖

your grey-green gaze

holds

my blue body

eight years old

we are

eight years old again

❖

playing clutch ’n grab streetball dream green lake, yellow dunes, purple clover—

your sweet wet heat

❖

fingers

petal

by

petal

we both look away

❖

your cut-glass voice

tell me

crystalline

❖

fissured

dolomite

seeptrickleflowrush   surface   surface   (you come

\   /   \

ground   slant

❖

narrative deconstruction

        (prepare my heart

       : retrospective lo...

the weight of

hello

the weight of

❖

lips|spil

here

& here

& here

❖

an open field—

space traversed by lines of

night ride

home

redemption

song

fall blue light, slant—

splayed soybean husks   (whiff of dry rot

❖

eye, heart, the field

contiguous

❖

strange

to want: (scraps)

to get what you want:

❖

dutch elm death

largo

peal *pianissimo*

❖

what were the odds?

big city; tangled skein of sub-

way; sliding doors: you

\

me

MORE FUN WITH 'PATAPHYSICS

Sharon Harris

Poets have a long history of being the first to discover the keys as to why we are the way we are. The findings are amazing, but to people who are not trained in meter and metaphor, understanding how poets arrive at these incredible discoveries is a mystery.

While poetic research is a complex and intense process, some of the steps leading to important discoveries can be done in your own home. Why not call up a friend to help?

7. Poets who lose their way.

Why do poets fly to the warm lights of pubs and bars? They are not naturally attracted to these places, but misled. Flying at night, poets steer by the moon. They know they are flying in a straight line as long as the moon shines into their eyes from the same side. But when they pass the lights of a public house, they get confused. They leave their straight flight path and approach in spirals.

8. If I place a poem and its translation across from each other, and I stand between them, can I see my reflection stretching away into infinity?

In theory, you could get an infinite number of reflections in the poems, but only if the poem was perfectly translated and you stood there forever.

124. Editing Poems

Fill a tall jar with water and place your latest poem in it. Try to drop words into the text. It is very surprising that however carefully you aim, the words nearly always slip to the side.

It is seldom possible to get a word to fall straight. The very slightest nuance with even the smallest tilt is enough to cause a greater resistance of the water on the slanting underside of the word. Because words are full of holes, they turn easily and drift out of context.

48. Why do poems sparkle?

Even if a poem looks rough, some of its very small parts can be smooth as a mirror. When light hits something smooth, it bounces. The more smooth parts the light has to bounce off, the more it sparkles. So poems with lots of little smooth bits really sparkle and shine.

59. What would happen to the world as we know it if poems were entirely hollow beneath their letterforms, assuming that they did not collapse inwards?

If poems were hollow, we would be in danger of death by suffocation, thirst, frying, starving, freezing and drowning – in that order.

11. What is poetry?

Poetry, a form of energy, is all around us. Even in a quiet place, you can hear poetry.

Poems are chambers through which sound is forced in order to study effects on ideas mounted within.

18. How do they make haikus look like haikus and sonnets look like sonnets?

In the poem factory, the stiff poem dough is pushed through the souls of special people called poets. The shape of the poem that comes out depends on the shape of the poet it was pushed through. When the dough is pushed through sensitive monastic poets, you get haikus. When it's pushed through Leo poets with Libra risings, you get sonnets.

15. Where's the best place to sit at a poetry reading?

Sit up front if you want the best view. Sit in the middle if you want a scary ride. Sit in the back to feel like you're floating.

174. What do poets think?

As far as I know, poets don't really think on the same level as we do, so answering your question is a bit tough. Poets don't have the same brain development, so they don't have a conscience or any of the other higher order functions. They can dream, however, and almost all of their daily activities are results of habit or instinct. You can train them by using the granting system, but you can't train them to think for themselves (without you, they can't figure out how to fill out their own grant applications, etc.).

Poets vaguely recognize things outside of their inner feelings, so it is difficult for them to form social hierarchies and relationships amongst themselves. If I were a poet, I probably would not think about my future or past at all, but just pay attention to what is happening right now.

111. Why should I not freeze a poem?

There is no reason that you should not freeze a poem that I am aware of.

143. Can a poem be too ironic?

Yes. Irony is a finite source for poetry; however, I am sorry to note that in a poet's life, irony is infinite.

EXPERIMENTS IN PROGRESS

Can I get warts from touching a poet? Do poets dream?

If I swallow my words, will they stay in my stomach for ten years?

Is life its own metaphor?

If a sound poet makes a funny face, will it be stuck forever?

How many poems would I have to write for the total to add up to $16?

STANDARD POSE

D.G. Jones

Vespers of Sorts

pipes and a snare drum

        music, ahem

a cat and a terrier ragging the end
of a cloudcapped day

what's left of it's now   is
a raggedy tartan the drone
drags away

The Bones Hang Out

the bones hang out
like armour and feathers, the corset
of mail, the bodice
with gold filigree

                    hang around
like the deaths of the stars

things in a closet

expressive

the fibula speaks to some drapery
fallen away

the codpiece or doublet
the heart
or tender of manhood

                              they are still
the rag and boneshop, ready
to put on the play

War and Peace

snow

the day shut down like Napoleon
at Moscow

a day for art

the marvel of flight and of stillness
commotion and silence: the medieval
Japanese paintings of war

the warriors
                birds, arrows, the armour
slatted, just like the feathers – all
flying with horses, what not, the pigments
over the centuries

lightly and deadly and pretty

nothing like it – well
maybe Duffy
the horses, jockeys, ladies with parasols

oh, the races in summer

oh, the summer in winter, the war
in art

Speed of Light

maybe children can live
at the speed of light

adults on the Infobahn burn
like meteors

walking too long in the wind
can you hear yourself think

it's an analgesic

blind in a blizzard and dazed
in the lull

angels do better, knowing
there's nowhere to go

like children, maybe, enjoying
getting there fast

For Molly Lamb Bobak

the concentration of flowers
and stems, their
liberation in air – or the wet
of the paper

                    did it mean
lambsquarters close to the ground
were but weeds of
the imagination

                    no
but colours were lacking: it's a question
of stacking the eyes with a solid
shimmer, the tones
falling, and rising

as if an architect built in a wash
a music of care

Ideas of the End of the World

the latest: a universe
losing its gravity

it will become its own
emanation
                    very thin, very cold, very dark
an enormous
unseeable haze

the forlorn bit of a juniper
stuck in a vase
looks almost abundant
                                        though tonight
I can see how it bends in a wind
I can't feel

a weak vehicle, yes, its tenor
vastation

Esoteric Beauty

snowdrops in sleet, a flank
exposed or
barely recovered
                    as if lace
or pearls in a tangle
of things decomposed were a

haute couture

like Miss Haversham's feast

like that word
algolagnia

in heat in the cold, a style
of grotesque
we call spring
                    like WCW's
"beautiful thing"

In the Fast Lane, and in Flowers

birds drop out of the sky

one peeled from a bumper
two fell from the glass
of a door, of a window

they no longer fly

this is full summer
birds quick in their death
flowers in their colour
                                        and I
with two cracked ribs
now quickened in leisure

– my fall arrested by a still
solid rafter

– how time flies, oh, yes
even at rest in the garden
and the measure ...

let's say it's like summer: the fullness
of changes
minute and extreme and at once
maybe only a leaf
maybe rain and a wind, maybe also
lightning and thunder

What Is Deep

is the body washed out of a river
a flint in the thigh
after 9,000 years

something constant
and grave

to ponder when filing the nails

like cremation

la donna e mobile
in the depths of the air

it's like white water rafting, a chasm
between sex and a haircut

the annual check-up

murder will out, as they say

And What's the Purpose of That?

the purpose of leaves is declining the light
from sunup to sundown

oh, the clouds, they too, but they are either
like old strong verbs from the Saxon
or the flimsiest stuff

the leaves are both dense and aerated, sensation
in endless inflection, like skin
swept by fear and delight

with something like bone, but mottled
or dark in interstices

changing and somehow the same

I think leaves are like hands, like an infinite
laying on of the hands

and sometimes they mutter like ancient
priests or nuns saying something
we don't understand
                                        except it's the music
of fear and of trembling

– then we get light nearly naked, examine
what fell, in strange shapes, all
warty and coloured, and not unlike, we think
our dearly departed

MY CITY IS ANCIENT AND FAMOUS (SPRAWL)

Julia Williams

it matters that we chose to live apart, confined by highways to our private habitats, that you always said it's quiet here (who could ask for more), that I bragged about my broken car, the muscles in my calves, the soothing caterwaul of noisy streets.

a private life

I want to build houses in the dusk
of a late century

mud pits smudged with human feet

shapely cusps

sawdust grain cupped in my eyes
soft drywall smooth on beams and posts

prism, window
gather inside

people are particles or people are waves
try sleeping alone, warm your feet on your own thighs
rub your own back
with your own hands

you must find a place for your feet

you are pedestrian

if you choose to romanticize footprints you can't protect your shoots

guard your grass and your skin

if you idealize human tracks you cannot love grass seed

you cannot naturalize boundaries

leave the wheelbarrow where it stands

for whimsy

Amanda and I watch construction. the ravine backed by money buckets with great rooms and mountain stone facades. the field they overlook is slated for a Costco, Amanda says. ha, six acres of parking lot and a warehouse for an expensive view? we hate wealthy people.

altitude gives me the bends
collapses my bread loaves
the inner ear: the saddle
a small matter of my brain
loosening

our old house had tree wallpaper and a milk chute, brown shag and a picture window. a snug bungalow too tight for the five of us. that was my parents' first house and they painted the garage door yellow and brown, bee stripes. in the new house they chose muted colours, off whites, details in wood and slate: adult.

when Amanda moved we were inspired. gathered brochures for a townhouse development, sunny grass islands, hidden garages. knowing we couldn't afford it we designed a home, input from family, formed a floor plan. by night Dan had a studio and I had an office, pine versus beech for kitchen cupboards, hmm. imaginary habitats.

This moment
A neighbourhood dwindles
its trees ash
one window velveted yellow

don't worry, this happens all the time
cracks in sidewalks, descriptions of gardens

stars mount the rooftops
moths butter porchlights
this is typical, probable
this is a description of perpetual events
in a simple, demarkable space

look from above: a rope of units
single pieces of tape
rake up these houses

This moment
maybe apples sweeten
maybe deals sweeten
but the sky gets no brighter
the clockhand no quicker

my city is an ancient and famous destination

it snows through april and grows dim
pavements ruin shoes and in our hands
matters gain gravity. if the sun would shine
we'd get along better

when it thaws this city smells of shit
throw parties and pretend daffodils
booming ice takes apart the water
a river eats itself

widen the streets for clarity
fill our days with puddles
our nights with ruined snow

the woman who works in urban planning said it wasn't the phone calls that upset her but the aldermen. they shake each other's hands and shred her plans. "that's not progress." what I noticed was the pale light on her cheeks, rings of torn flesh around her fingernails, the softness of her desk-bound body.

you can't join the community association if your house is on Tuscarora Close. something to do with developers, just the way it goes. Amanda's neighbours can't use wrenches or saws, make crooked steps and ascend bent all summer. makes no sense. she keeps a level head.

remind me that the street hasn't licked us yet

congruent squares and triangles equal nothing

no one is crooked around here. that's why it's safe for kids to be kids

architects are most interested in space *between* houses

what I wanted, said the urban planning woman, was a window I could look out and see things grow

I wasn't raised to pile humans

the end of my parents' street was a mound of dirt
lawns barbered to fine stubble, trees fine as hairs

I retreat from close talkers, touchers
won't suffer middle seats or wall sides of beds
let me wave my legs
I come from room to swing a cat, to shout
sound off: unhuman space

the house turned eighteen. when it was a mud lot Dad took a photo of the three of us perched in a backhoe shovel. he drilled extra screws into the floorboards so they wouldn't squeak. we swept sawdust off the edge of the living room, down to the mud puddles and splinters of wood. wet concrete, glue smell, sawdust. eighteen years later the floors squeak anyway, but less.

snow on sandstone walls. last night
the city froze a waxy blue
red shapes blossomed in my cheeks
my blood here, and my language

we don't hear birds here. the air
is white and hazy with our voices
I saw moisture from my lungs
hang from my eyelashes and ears

touch nothing and don't pause. this city
contracts and crackles on itself
snaps bright pieces off our lives
explains our bodies to us, our most simple sounds

snowed under again, hedging

imagine hiding glass in the carrot tops
imagine creosoting the fence

trespasser or transgressor, whatever
it all means passing through

we live all the time between lines

in the new house we didn't have a fence, we had rabbits, cats, porcupine. Mum pre-painted slats and Dad nailed them, cementing each post in the ground. fawn trimmed with oxford brown. now it's brown.

if you often interpret silence
you know noise vibrates
and the violent can't be soothed by empty rooms

this makes sense
we cloak the streetlights to confound moths
this makes sense
we wear masks to underscore our basic authority

loud voices remind me of engines
remind the masked they are visible
sound gathers in fabric, but bends in water
peels our eardrums
moves us closer to our doors

there were tragedies on the street
cars into houses, cars into toddlers
can't combat black ice, like black death
a sore on these radiant streets

asylum at front porches, block parents
lilies wilt on shaven lawns

water restrictions are voluntary but noble

to combat the weather build bodies
no weather can crack

Amanda and I like to drive through Mount Royal. we admire the properties, the expense, the upkeep. it always comes down to one of us saying, imagine cleaning that! comments like these keep us in our place.

NORTHEAST ANTI-GHAZALS

Eric Folsom

Northeast

If you picked any story but this,
I wouldn't know where to begin.

The grey November sky predicting early snow,
The ground already resisting footprints.

A young doe in my garden looks up;
How the mind seeing, loses sight.

Inside where I stand, one cobweb on the ceiling
Delicately twists when the furnace comes to life.

What if I turned my face away
And when I looked back you were gone?

The freezing mud in the driveway
Seizes the tires in their ruts overnight.

I wish for multiple eyes like a spider,
My forehead of shining cobblestones.

Sexual Response

Sex in the morning before the children woke up,
I began writing stories about love in my journal.

He could see a strange car in the driveway
And knew right away something was wrong.

Only a trip to Toronto, he'd said;
No reason not to believe him.

I was reading an article about Vietnam,
With a two year old sleeping sweetly on my lap.

He pictured the hawk soaring above the valley,
Heard stillness except for a far highway.

Her letter arrived later the same day:
"He follows me everywhere, a jealous animal."

I remember she brought me clothes for dancing in,
She poured the wine while I prepared the food.

The Wise

She wore a scent like blue light bulbs,
Wore her coat the way trees wear hills.

After the bloodiest campaign in years,
His heart smouldered like an old cigar.

His eyes put down roots for the first time,
The light of crows in his hair.

Every influence caught her off-guard:
A vaginal infection, the phone calls.

He courted his own grief,
He thought she would be his second wife.

No angry objects on this table,
No jack-in-the-box anger from your lips.

I love your failure to communicate,
I love your naked back facing me.

Just Another Yuppie Raising Children

When the lights came on, our apartment
Had been reborn as a red hibiscus.

In those days everything went into my journals,
Each ordinary discovery about love and children.

The sweetness of our cumulative sleep deficit;
The baby woke again, and we danced with her till dawn.

I said to my anti-war friends: we've won,
Don't you see they're getting old and dying?

Weighing the hour in my chapped hands,
I borrowed the lanolin you bought for your breasts.

Labouring with love for love, the wedding ring
On the spice shelves while I do the dishes.

Reservations

The long turbines of history, sometimes a city
Rehearses before the plane touches down.

Your black beret with sequins, the lost earring,
The tickets torn in half, dropped in the wastebasket.

Tell them this is your life and the world
Will fit only one way, your double helix.

These passenger jets, enormous dancers,
Peeling away from the heat haze on the ground.

The runways were built on harbour landfill,
Old cars, rubble, and a broken television.

Judge your time by the very darkest
Red flower. Your table is waiting.

He Waits In the Oak Panelled Library

The brass asp coiled on a leather-bound book;
His son is grateful for a glass of sherry.

Temperatures are falling throughout the Midwest;
Tonight the river returns to its beginning.

Black horses huddled in the snow-covered field,
His leather raincoat, his long hair.

When bridges wash away the gas lines rupture,
That is the future of passion.

A silvery package does the real work,
Keeps us all dancing over the ocean.

He has a scar across his forehead,
She raises her skirts to pass safely over flames.

All the Way to 93

The human body as a reference tool: appendix
At the back of a book, hands on the clock.

The earth circles the sun so much faster;
Even when we fly, we're crawling.

Main arteries inbound are backed up
All the way to 93.

More of us is, beside an apple tree
And an old stone farmhouse in Quebec.

Of course services are vastly better;
Medicine comma, television exclamation mark.

The cat watches us depart, her ears laid back,
Poised for a burst of imagery.

The Gore

Clay mud whitens as it dries on the tires,
Patterned grooves left in the driveway.

Beyond the last field, a dense swamp under starlight;
He calls them coyotes, wild dogs his own answers.

Strength enough left to shore up the old house,
He knows that old barns fall down mainly at night.

Next farm west, facing the highway,
The big sign announces a planned community.

No fish could live in a stream this small,
Though salmon were once plentiful in the harbour.

If he looks sharp, he sees a fox
Cutting through his orchard in the morning.

This cup is full, so easy to spill;
No love without wanting, no power without control.

Slipping Away

Whatever lies frozen in the ice, a mitten or a Buick,
Suspended as though floating upside down in the sky.

The fiddle music over, so the priest went home
And saw the ghost of his father sitting on the bed.

Late in the season when the ice gets soft,
Some drunk tries to cross at night and disappears.

Most people worry about saying the wrong thing,
Think too long about the darkness beneath their feet.

Wheels lock automatically
When passenger doors are open.

She gave her daughter the red sweater and a key
To the safety deposit box down at the bank.

Something that shouldn't have been there,
A car in the same spot for days, gathering tickets.

Natural History

"Create with form, not line," said the art teacher,
"build with masses of light and dark."

Gradually plants evolved from gymnosperm to seed
And the Age of Flowers dawned on the Earth.

I forget the dead sometimes, leave them out of poems,
And they come back in dreams to remind me.

My grandmother spoke to me when I was nine,
"You won't forget your mother will you?"

The seeds of the new plants made concentrated food,
Allowing birds and mammals to evolve and flourish.

I'm running out of energy, lesson plan falling apart;
"What do we mean," I say twice, "by economy?"

Any world is dangerous and filled with metaphor:
The burning lasers of our eyes, fatal wounds of birth.

In Spite of Everything

Mission Control is a room full of males;
So many in one place, you feel proud or afraid.

Unsealing the travelogue with one hand,
He knows how to pack a suitcase, even room for a heart.

The gossip of written culture, this lateral pass;
A billboard driven by cubist engines turns to greet us.

Where is Bly's old path bordered by seashells?
Choking with rage tonight, 60% chance of rain.

The evidence of water's path in the stone,
A fine line becoming a crack, becoming a chasm.

A hummingbird's egg, the size of a baby's thumbnail;
The police in the woods with a metal detector.

Travel Poem

In a park in a foreign city, the geese feed together,
The single swan strikes a pose near the pond.

Like a laser operation to repair a torn retina,
The sun glints precisely off an office building.

One famous painter sees this town through pain,
The broken glasses of childhood, and redeems it.

I write too much, revise too long;
The wife who waits, gives up and goes to bed.

To be remembered for our briefest encounters;
The young poet romances an island, then sails away.

As the moon rose, I drove the rented car
With my children asleep in the backseat.

Taxtime Poem

Your bricks lining the edge of the garden,
Your house moving through the storm.

I no longer know who I am when alone:
Am I making breakfast for you or for us?

The hissing of cars along a rainy street;
The tax office is open, the gift shop is closed.

A little girl at lunchtime shows me her umbrella;

"See, I can open it," she pulls on one end.
I object to this metallic odour,
Yet I'd fade away if the system died.

Smarties on the floor, rolling under the fridge;
Her bright look, a glimmer of a smile, then gone.

ReSet

Breakfast of shouting and spilled cereal;
Coffee waits until the children change clothes.

The snow drifts in smooth aerodynamic shapes;
My car is a spaceship, I am released from routine.

No school either, everyone shovels.
When the driveway is clean, the plow comes.

Never push the reset button more than once;
It's a mistake to believe your life is under control.

The smell of spices in the kitchen where she irons,
Friends and relatives like a fabric over the city.

I walk down the middle of life's snowy road,
A child at each hand, and the snowplow is coming.

Birthday Poem

A voice calling from the children's room,
Telling what the birds are doing this morning.

A woman carries heaven in her lips;
The robin gathers dried grass in its beak.

The need to create this family, the desire
To make a birthday cake in the shape of a four.

The wind is cool on my child's bare legs
As he lets the bicycle glide along the pavement.

Searching for clues in the birthday treasure hunt,
We come to the garden, where lilacs bloom.

That night we dreamt of stars and fountains,
Coloured fireworks expanding above our heads.

We were part of the third body, larger than ourselves
Commanding us to wake up and make love.

THE CULT OF DAVID THOMPSON.

Gregory Betts

"I am a solitary traveller"

precanada askd young Thompson, carve the border, make us, divide us from the rest, walk the ice and survey and write the land...

"This place was to me a new world... who can tell what has passd here in ancient times?"

he travelld 70,000 kays on foot, by canoe, most often alone. listend hard. when we walk in canada, we walk his shadow. when we are canada, we are near his knife.

Jan 1

i step into the sky, my
feet barely touch the hill

suddenly

i am an unheard word
spoken by the night

i try to listen, i can hear it,

- somewhere -

but can not say it

in cool woods, i
make tea on stray embers
and a fire glow
thinking
someone must love me at home

thinking further

i don't know home
i don't know where home is

Sonnet One

To paint a country:
carve your canvas from the earth
drip wet colour portraits of the sky
divided trees, divided eyes

whereever i paint
is
This or There

And I Know Neither!

the rib cage of the world
is not always smooth
not always loud, not always seen

who hides in these forest bones?
who uses them for what
(w)here?

me defining nations
unknown to me, unknown

Jan 6

the snow is

this snow, that snow

very snow, big snow

snowy snow

[someone says, hard pack, ice-crust
angel light
duster ice, man killing, the drift,
swallowing one big evanescence...]

where here there is pure white, but what will the snow know *there*
beyond C, when my colour falters, lies, will there will be pure white
when i make C, what of the water's song?

but
the snow will always remember those songs
will haunt us with memory

Jan 8

I walk, carve, the dogs
follow, lead, tumble

break fresh snow

we break to kill rabbits
and I get none of it
sometimes the dogs think for me

but i have not learned their tongue
only the murmur of unquiet
moon eyes and hunger
  behind my eyes

if I didn't take some pleasure
in going hungry, I would
be a clerk, by now

somewhere in london
lying down in folded newsprint, my soul untouched
undisturbed

instead i am here in infinity
and who but me remembers how to get here?

news comes to me in vague gestures
from fur clad strangers, that disappear
in packs or fade into swallowing   cedars
the ribs of the earth

shadows and soft threats between A and C, it goes back and forth
    hear the faint pulse of B the shadow of R and of
G, an endless saga, a distraction
a fool's game.   i am doing something different

i turn around again, see snow. there are no footprints
      up ahead, tho many shadows leave a whispering trace

sometimes i hear things
the dogs can't
sometimes i write these things
down, read them alone by the fire
drinking willow bark tea

sometimes i can't don't
sometimes i just walk thru
that noise
beyond imagination, before fact

Jan 11

Three As and an I
eating raw bull and grazing
 the languid silence, as i cut
my line around them
      they askd if they had to move

i pull my country so it
stretches round them, eats the fire
    sit down in C, now, and eat together

i always eat in C, i tell them
Well, we like to sleep and piss in A,
                three told me

       the I presumes not to spell

i undo the countries.
There, i say. Tonight we eat, sleep, and piss
                free

                        sit down silent
                  listen to stories and the wind
                              all night.

                morning. they are gone.
                 i and i in my country
                        alone with my knife

Jan 30

where am i?
where is it?
where am i?

can't remember where
  the dogs buried themselves

but the wind is a new canvas
  stretching over my

snowd in ears
snow din
snow dinner
                    no dinner, again

Sonnet Two

freeze
i leave the pale
trail for a sideways
breeze

i and i
now bone
find a lone
quiet sound

lie hearing how loud
my breath and that cloud

The Scarlet Hunter Came to me

The Scarlet Hunter came to me
in the night
He was fire   smoke
 Coyote's eye and a beard that flowed
Around the wild armed trees.

He said, "D you will die here, but
not now. Not when the woods tremble at your knife. They will grow to hate you
before this earth will take you."

He told me where *here* was
and i listend thru
curlish winds of snow

His eyes in the night sky,
His robe smoothing the world, his eyes
twirling with ravenous colour,
everywhere

i can never be alone with myself
anymore

Feb 2

my knife thru the
 throat of a thump dazd buck
  i eat all day, awaken lifeless blood,
   and extend myself.
  Carry meat, skin
  until i find the village

Sacrifice

Eyes follow me from the frozen bush
They are all around me
Wondering why my dogs act so crazd
Wondering what for

i say, in my head, *Kisiskatchewan*
i say, out loud, *Please welcome me*

Feb 13

my finger is black
 cold chewing to the bone
 i did not notice until
i thot
  Musketoes and Sand flies
 had crawld thru my gloves.

i need a village. i'm losing.
i can feel the Scarlet Hunter walking
  two steps back,

he is not pleasd with me

i watch him each night
hunched over my buried
dogs whispering in the
buried boreal sky

licking his lips

he knows i hear this whispering

it is my curse

Sonnet: My Mouth

my mouth froze
closd today
from a leaking nose
and a dry frozen sky

Learning not to hate
cold
holding fear
letting fear burn for me

i don't let the dogs lie for sleep, anymore
we are all just seconds away from death, SH,
my God, i still hope

Feb 16

i can't see nothing
thru snow

it is all white
i have to stop

i've lost every dog, every thing
but my knife

i have to stop

fatd into facing the faceless

Feb 18

People elude me, storms confound me,
i talk to myself, eat my own mind,

i fall everywhere,
Nothing ends
  the sky, here, the snow,
 why can't i say the snow?
i have no other thoughts

It's eating me, i need the village,
  i need more shelter
 i need the secret,
 i need you to leave me, fiendish eyes,
i'm not ready to die

i have nothing to confess

Feb 20

wind and snowd all day
made travel very bad
snow suckld my boots
like reluctant lovers

            suddenly surroundd

flat, flat lands
i can see forever
i can see the hope of
the village
  that eludes me,
lost in the crimson cloak of SH

i have managd to avoid the abyss
by the warm breath of my shadow
 we walkd the creature's edge
and murmur mad comforts at each loss

my spirit falters, blaming me for eating
  the buried
dogs i could catch
I confess without knowing
Nor knowing that I have any limits left
But the want to live

I keep hearing
something
 a creature, not human
  yet surely of us,
watching taking down these stories,
who is the shadows on the outside of being,
to whom the dogs howl
  the winds crawl the earth
 beneath the snow
 above the green blue light sky
 above the canoe lake
 buried with my broken dogs

From whom men hide their heads
  in their own inventions
and sometimes fall silent to hear

the sun is a minataur in these flat lands
galloping hastefully thru
the bull-hornd clouds
burning your eyes blind-black mirrors
with its sacred glance

everything is now a squint

Samuel Hearne's House

some way, i make it.
Into the arms of a
soul filld house,
drumskins stretch my ears
stretch with warmth and welcome; i'm already falling away

but this is SH's house,
this is his world that i,
the listening dead, walk thru now

wendigo whispers outside
human stories with every snowflake

WRITING THE WRITING

Natalie Simpson

Writing the writing that should enter into conversation but clips the door frame again and again.

The writing that sounds out numbered, or weary.

The writing that looks for the right kind of note book and can't see itself on scrap.

Writing that all smug has to go.

Writing holds sound hostage.

Writing from form to formal.

The writing content to lie.

Writing that speaks out each side of the mouth it imagines.

Writing on lost time cringes and moon.

Writing stitches sound to page.

The writing that flummoxes all fakes.

The method of writing that lets the reader know where the writer began and where the reader should go.

The writing that would press its naked flesh against the fenestration.

Wiring gets crossed and sparks. Writing gets lopped.

Gets loopy and long-winded or stops.

Writing chaw slop jam in the jaw. Writing that frets all five but mostly why?

Please, the writing wants to say, please stay.

The writing whose time has come.

Personified writing or merely sonified.

Writing that can't make words new just makes new words.

Writing doesn't get out much or does get out, but doesn't like what it sees; writing recedes and writing seethes.

Writing in a closed system.

Or a clothes closet.

Writing in a dark room.

Writing dank moon.Writing suspicious integers.

Writing well aware.

That writing slowly changes colours in the fall.

At this writing could still be relevant.

Some writing self-effaces.

Writing should get its facts straight.

This writing can't stand you.

Most writing would like to advance a theory of punctuation correlative to.

At this writing, writing comes and goes.

There is always a writing that would like to define writing, and there is always a writing that would like to defy writing.

Come on, you might say to writing, you can't be serious.

Equally, the writing might find you out.

It all comes out in writing.

Many people are writing right now and will be anyway.

Some are wondering about writing and some are just writing.

Writing about can be at odds with writing for and writing to.

Writing to and fro.

There is writing that is a method of discovery and there is writing that is a method of coercion.

There is blunt writing and writing struck through.

Is writing present tense affectation; is writing past a fancy trick?

Writing a lovely linear.

Writing I could kiss you.

Then writing I won't.

The influence of the keyboard on writing, the influence of the PC on writing, the influence of writing on the habit of not writing.

The only time writing gets it sway.

Once in a while writing over arches.

Arch writing is a fashion.

Writing stakes a claim in the outcome, but writing is never as good as its word.

CUBA A BOOK

Monty Reid

People are fucking in the ruins of the recent past.
Lisa Robertson

Imagination
always has a body.

Revolution always
has a boat.

You have entered
the black room

and the celebrated boat
is preserved

in a glass house
in the old city.

Description
is no longer possible.

What's left
of the sea

has never
arrived.

There is no point
in waiting any longer.

Undo
what remains

of your clothes
what remains

of the waves.
Out at the warp

light begins
its necessary travel

It is headed towards you
like a boatload

of hungry

just hungry.

The road opens

Reluctantly
wedge of headlights

a man running
through the low-lying fog

into darkness.

Pot-holes
soldiers and barricades

on the airport road
checking the papers

hard stabs of light
that doubt

who you are.
Oh yes

we are still
who the papers

say we are.

A cloud of jellyfish
wash up

on the shore
at Santa Maria

where you found
a cheap hotel

built by the Russians
and used

as a love hotel
in their idyllic phase

and then abandoned
in the general

abandonment
that comes after

the idyllic phase.
The jellyfish tremble

in the small breeze
or is it resentment

since no one
will touch them

in spite of their beauty
and their arms

so many, so much
to let go of

can still
hurt you.

Remember
the Russians?

How they went
home disappointed

in love
and in concrete?

Step out of
your blue step-in

wrap
please

the one I had not seen
before

step out of the tankini
with scooped legs

What is that smell
on you?

Stand here
on the cold tiles.

All night the revealed
leaches into the built

world, mortar crumbles
in the walls.

Out where the light
warps

through the ironic
atmospheres

and the postcard
colors attach

everything else
has already floated away.

The waves have all
abandoned something

and yet they arrive
with that coating

that gel
of surfaces

at the exact location
of the body, at

your toes
to be more specific

which you painted
so carefully

yesterday afternoon
wedging them apart

because they can't
be trusted together.

Everyone
is who they say

they are.
Is.

The radicals
make a singular

narrative
in the glass house

patrolled
by their infantry

and their angels.

You can see
in.

They must be
as beautiful

as they say they
is.

So just arriving
doesn't prove anything

except that it was past
midnight

and even so
I had to wake you

didn't I?
Where did the notion

of the subject
as free ever come from?

Or the free market
for that matter.

Down past the salsa bar
and the palms hatching

out of their long tubes
is the black spume

of darkness
on the beach

Take me there
and fuck me silly.

My cock was still
slick with you

that first morning
early

streaks of light
across the bed

and in the hallway
a gas motor fires up.

Two boys
in red t-shirts

and a gas-fired
bazooka

at the door
to disinfect us

Huh?

Dengue fever
in the mangrove swamps

mats of algae, larval stages, shifts of
hot particles

and right at the beginning
of tourist season too.

So the volunteers in red t-shirts
come room to room in mid-morning

expecting everyone to be gone
to the beach or the old city

and purify every room
then slam the door

to let purity take
its effect.

When you return
you can feel its residue

on all the surfaces
and wonder

what's that smell.

So we are pure
briefly

but the breakfasts I hear
are always the same

dry toast and coffee
and an omelette

with onions and if
they have it today

some hard grated cheese
shortages

in the background.
There is no excess here

no surplus, no more
to life

than what it contains
and just the right amount

of bananas.

That was our first morning
in Santa Maria

after that we were up early
and out of the room

What exits, what
displaces

what a breath was
when it's gone.

Is everything
endlessly finite?

Maybe that's just the feeling
you get on an island

finitude I mean

so many steps
down to the beach

in any direction
smoke lifting from

canefields on the other
side of the freeway

and a single cloud
fraying in the sunlight

then another one
over in direction

of Guanabao

The glued-together
vintage cars

with their fold-up
wings drift

along the wet streets.
It made you remember

going out with guys
in cars like that

Crown Vics and Desotos.
Since they can't get

parts
they drop in Lada motors

and keep them running
because they'd

all rather drive cars
you remember making out in.

Maybe that's why
I have begun to think

rusted-out Ladas
are the only true vehicles

of the revolution.
We could put bullet-holes

Among the densely-packed
and celebrated tombs

the living
find their way

with difficulty.
Some are here

the old man explained
to pray for fertility

they touch the marker
leave their flowers

on the slab
and find their way

back to the street.

And some are here
to pray for love.

Which tomb do they go
to that for?

Oh, almost all of them
he said.

Were you as lonely
as CNN

left on in an
empty room?

With the sound
turned down?

The European
edition?

With South American
weather?

And dowdy
anchor people?

And the room
looks like it's full

of water?
And still

there was no news.
Me too.

And what is it
I'm doing here?

Among the maximum utility
of the sites.

At the cemetery.
Among the cannons.

Too old now
to be following someone

to Los Corales
the hotel once painted

electric blue
now spalling down

to the poorly-constituted
grey concrete

residue of everywhere.
I thought I could just

find you
among the fatigue

of surfaces
but I couldn't.

I thought I could just
wait for you

at the frictions of meaning
but I couldn't.

The rooms
crumble around us.

In order to describe
you have to embrace.

This is why
I'm a tourist.

Not a pilgrim.
Not a traveler.

Not a nomad.
All that neo

liberal posturing.
Once you unfold

the map
you can't get it

folded back up
again.

Before dawn
I stand on the balcony

with its broken plaster
and watch the salsa

band pack up
at the bar across the street.

Not that they have much
to pack.

Conga, claves, tres.
To make the world

is to listen.
The room

where you will remain
smells of routine

music, your face

pressed into
the threadbare sheets

a small wind
of chemicals leaching

into the concrete
destroying it.

THE BLACK PRINCE OF BANK STREET

William Hawkins

A Pimping Analogy

Donna was a cocksucker
Working the street
Out Hintonburg way
Until she saw the light. And,
By God, the light was bright!
It flashed, heading east to west,
Almost atomic in it's glare,
So startling to Donna.
She did declare, I've had it—
I'm out of here.
She walks the streets
For Jesus now
And Jesus loves her
Don't you know!

Not Here, Not There

I don't know why there's no love in my life,
She said, her arms outstretched querulous,
But pleading.

I don't mean sex, but it all seems
So far away, so very far away.

I just can't get there.

King Kong Goes To The Shawville Fair

O I went to the Shawville Fair
Hoping to find other Beasties there.
Alas there were none!
But still I had fun
Getting drunk with raccoons
On stale beer.

Constance Maureen

Thing of beauty
Nothing is forever,
I've seen so much sizzle fade,
But my love for you will never
Be enticed to degrade
Until forever is nothing,
And beauty a thing

The End Of The Line

Being drunk, looking down the track,
Waiting for the big train,
Muttering about
An absence of light.

Being sober, looking down the track,
Waiting for the big train,
Wondering why
It's suddenly so bright.

Can I Have This Dance?

So soft of skin, yet harsh of voice—we so
Trapped by the poverty of our aspirations
And capabilities. Limited by our
Loveless dance. Going round
The empty dance floor
One more time.

Do you love me?
(I can barely move)
Do you love me?
(Now I've lost my groove)
Do you love me?
(Now that I can't dance)

Maybe Somebody Will Email

Maybe somebody will email
A lonely old man
Who remembers what he wants
And forgets what he can.

Or some sweet thing from the past
Will call & recall things too good to last.
A day of sunshine, full of love,
Ending with dark clouds roiling above.

Birthday Poem

I used to be a star
And when I came out at night
Folks would gather round
And say, my God his light is bright.

But then my light faded
And things are not the same
When I come out at night
They say, what the fuck's his name.

Elegy For Everybody

How strange this growing attachment
To minor keys, or a lonely dog's forlorn
Howling in the prison of a yard;
You can try not to hear it, but then you start to feel it
Echoing in the winter street.

How wonderful is the sunshine
When observed from the shade...
Or seen from the cool dark
Of a personal cave.

Blues Shuffle

We're all old men now,
Have become what we professed to hate,
Wheezing our way, searching out
Those mythical bargains
For unavailable dollars.

Downhill Fleeting

My poor old son, what have you done?
Gone all large, losing
The youthful exuberance,
Encumbered by curses real &
Genetic. Surrounded by mountains
Of snow. Nowhere to go but down,
Down those slippery slopes. Can I come too?

The Return

I saw you in a dream, &
You as real as twenty year ago
Except the hair, not corn-yellow,
But black. Warm eyes
Gone cold. But, hey, as the song say,
Got that old feeling, and am going
To run with it.

I can almost feel the soft hair
As it falls through my fingers ...

Another Day

For Marilyn

Nearly, no let us say every
Day when I think of you,
Hoping you stay well,
For you enclose my old
Man love/lust in your shoulders, in your arms;
As Jesus said if lustily looking
You become, commit & remain, as
I am, adulterously yours
Darling girl.

I'll see you in my schemes.

Thinking of Cobwebs

For Nelson Ball

When they came they were huge,
Spinning crazily downward—large
Like a giant's hand—
Grabbing folks
And calling them spiders.

Snowflakes, snowflakes,
Evil mutants
That are inclined to melt.

]

& LOOK THERE GOES A SPARROW TRANSPLANTING SOIL

] [3 ECLOGUES]

Emily Carr

1. begin & cease, to doubt

] I in the hinge [

weedless concrete & the softclicking louvred billboard

] statues, fountains, palm trees

]

(now again, trees)

greener than grass

cheerful prosthetics in the atmosphere of logo

] exhausted

] accidental

]

beauty

] .ordinary melodramatic.the melodramatic ordinary. [

nostalgia is another name for]

] hurrying after it

alive

] I moving about [unrolled

peeling an orange in El Salvador

] a macho guerilla fighter

the VP

of standard oil saying

] she or he

Cixous

in an ermine coat] a minor disaster of static

] the adjective deflects violence from the attention of the noun [

like Niagarafalls, or honeymoon [

]
the ozone smelling of violets
]

] plastic bags in concrete trees

]

]
unmappable
]
]

clouds

] the clayey smell of sun wounding wet concrete

]
] the hollow
twang of cheap champagne

a plastic heart strung on fishing wire [

]
& look there goes
a sparrow transplanting soil
]

2. o spare o spare o spare o

] nostos [

first, she must kill the house the sacred

]
]
story ermine as emancipation
embedded in landscape

]
]

become nobody's child owe no one nothing

] sign/ on the dotted line

a match burning in a crocus

] a sparrow flies downslope the Pizza Hut

]
]

in the hollow twang of neon
]
magnified shrapnel of interior sound

a housewife letting her wings down

] & virginia she stands there letting the words fall [

]
on/off, yes/no
]
like spring melt splosh the soft syllables
hotdog & orangesoda spill from the vendor's lips

if by yes/ you mean
]
]
ceasing to recognize herself:

crippled swings swagger from cowboy hats
turned inside out, emptied

]
then it was spring:
or no, it was winter
ending
]
a duet in which there is no dominant gesture
hopelessly mocking the ones who truly believe

traffic hums, a sparrow struts with a peanut

falling is easier
] yes
a matter of gravity
]
flesh unfurls

strangled [in the overlap

at the end of another scrapedout [
with merchandise agog
] you emerge from the photobooth with
]
] yourself in triplicate
]
breathe in breathe out

not knowing [the difference
] honks scatter like hailstones the sky
tears away
a piano plunges in the left margin
]
]
] facts
coming loose [from Styrofoam cups

] in the spray of red halogen [

flesh & bone smasht to atoms
] spring [

raking the asphalt & gurgling
] in the ruts

]
there is something missing
something like a wing] some fragment

] the crow's black eye on a white triangle
torn from envelope
]
]

3. turn

] subject of regret and absurd as well on the face of it [

] one hundred twenty pounds of melodramatic] ordinary

] masquerading as heroic

] feminine subject onomatopoeic
intransitive
dotted lines bone structures
dissolving

]
]
into landscape

] freshly bulldozered
childsafe [with an abstraction] she

in a velour hat & spider veil, the once-blush [of a past
which possibly had [ceased to exist
] as a present before entering
the present tense

] looking at] like [what
shall I [say how is the truth to be [said
believe me I [

] scorned as timber, beloved of the sky [

what merits celebration[

in the going which is always one
foot in front of the other [ ] panacea of same old
grafting landscape [
] into psychology

] you dont look old
]
]
] well I dont look] my age

] well you dont want to look
18 again do you [

]
]

] stilletoed spaghetti strapped bare backed

girlhood is a dying economy [
] happily comes into the world & there it is

Constance Witherby's statue disappearing
in snowdrift
shadows dropping from mailboxes [

] a moment of accelerated

hellbent
]
] flush with the curb

] the body comes undone [& spill:

right side lower arm raise arm bend knees repeat on left [

]
look,
like this line, breaking
even as it falls

a city bus says we'll pay you to read this ad
a severed hand blinks in treeshadow

sorry,
Eve said, to be a woman
]
]
ferrying corn on the hoof now pigs in a barrel
the Swanson man lifts a finger, honks

palimpsest of cut
adrift, alone (meat draped
] over bone

APARTMENTS, SECTION THREE

Aaron Tucker

LI.

when machines shift context
rust or rest the gap that spreads
is a change in function
it is here that synapses return
to limestone, water rises again

the hole is a place of entry
pore in tissue where
permeation seeps the single
preposition that pinpoints
adjective and within that phrase
the needless detail emerges

it is important then to fight
against the initial impulse to fill

the city is connective a laneway
as corruptible as a bypass, sluices these
houses are joined by joint trash pickup
and similar articles the pinpoints home
the specific is just as percolated as
general grid of blocks and turning lanes

but if space is medium then
the hole remains as fresh formed oolite

gaps as simple as a crack or
doorway a pedestrian lane, a detail
that keeps hides surreal, a secret

the new wound a pile of soft dirt
or decaying factory, a vocabulary lost
the natural urge is to seal this scar
to simply eradicate the cut
patch with concrete or low lying
coffee shops to heal with an adverb
quickly or persistently and let the body clot

but we must not be frightened by
this fresh space the daily unfamiliar that
we've gazed upon like lapping waves
but instead embrace it by constructing
light borders around protecting then entering

LIV.

the city crowds along
free morphemes and synthetics
then assembles its selves
on or in swarming locators
and reverses angles of adpositions

frames of reference determine
each body and its corresponding
grapheme bound to parameters
of downspouts alloy and fiberglass
each spatial each a subdomain ultimately
pointing towards a low ratio of
formative roots and limber joints

then we build onto or off of or over
the additions we make for clarity
of function hurried steely suffixes

and so we find places in that
where bodily coordinates
matter more, where structures are
fusional, those spaces where
angles of observation are unique, hopeful

LV.

the exact shape is unimportant if
one can be reformed into the other
a local detail like a freckle on her
midback traced in s (class 2 equal to u or h) shapes
landscape of skinny two lane streets
bumping underneath skin, an anatomy
he's familiar with vegetation, a city he's grown back to
a reflected pattern geometric but
still dependant on curvatures of movement
and puddle reflections kinetic traffic
grass growing back in spring around greys

(topology/topography)

LVI.

we're built

each in reference

LX.

closed curtains
tense and glimpse
furniture bodies
backlit recognizable
breathe
sidetable arm her doorway spine
window
tea cup breath joint and
instinctually mutual

LXI.

we conflate, each up tandem escalators
absorb into then we echo in sinuous rhyme
and only where a wall is broken we pause

exposed, the cell is open the interior
of walls spill out in concrete gulps
or pink fibers forgotten hidden wallpaper
or lost coins heating vents leak
dust we count the layers like tree rings
and number the events here the seasons
either light or dark and we can almost
build the skin of a sentence here
a telling that explains this wall

we gaze inward but now also outward
neither dominant ex and in equal parts
subject and object now share the same
intersect neither familiar or established

we recycle this space give texture back
absorb allow multiple meanings to structure
conflate we to he or she to us here

LXIII.

small hook of skin where his hip meets socket
low rise central renovated and large balcony

trace thighs hairy but smooth direct top of quads
carpeted floors air conditioning and fresh paint

her palm, back of his calf fingers molded to bulge
big bay windows facing morning sun bright kitchenette

then ankle the arch of foot linger vein pulses across
finger-smudged doors but ripening tomato plant

light back muscles crowd spine dig fingers there she
tea light candles on sill sunglasses wallet newspaper

finds his neck he collarbone tender gap to shoulder
handwritten note, pen, scratched table, half glass of water

exterior quiet neighborhood streets re
hair on soap fingernail clippings

angled roofs peaks thin wrist bones delicate
and scars organic and places to inhabit

XLIV.

for Ernest Burgess

we do not live in nesting dolls
circles that fit snugly within
we are not circles but tree rings
our center is not the heart
but the stomach lower intestine
proportional cubits from navel

of course, the heart is fluid, found
in long veins of water that runs along
shorelines where buildings perch
gaze in at beaches yearning for waves

we do not revolve around a center
we are not going downtown to do business
instead we live there in our holes
each nuclei each scribbling space
amorphously stretches outward
allows expansion of interior
with the shallow rise of each chest or voice

we live here in water our ocean is a lake or river
we are stones dropped in the center
we are subordinating pulsing in rings
and everyone a voyeur at window or shore edges

we watch, awash in etymology
aware of the impossibility
of touching each cell in the city

and so we are left with unknowing
the too large expanse that pushes
city limits suburbs sublime

or it is tiny in our corners so we repeat
syllables are ours again
syllables are ours again

LXV.

and later that night they tangle into each other on the floor or bathroom counter celebrating gleeful as their fingers are streets interlocking in grids their nails are front facing porches they are cells we are whole neighborhoods they are blending they are forming whole cityscapes as we intertwine the honks of cars and spare conversations drifting in through the window over the bed the covers knot at the bottom of the bed each a body each repetitive each a city to themselves each a city together

FRANK ST.

Cameron Anstee

The house you've sat in for years remains
against all odds,
                                a part of the earth.

George Bowering, *Kerrisdale Elegies*

                                                    Let
how I loved to be here
not change.

David O'Meara, "A Last Walk"

For Jenn, who found it & lives here.

I.

the building's foundation, slowly
giving way to one hundred years & more

I will never be older than this room

large enough to hold our books
but we'll move any way away from here

I know how this works
a thin, fine crack along several walls

Frank St. runs one way
Frank St. runs out of the canal

II.

a city folded into a river,
a canal, an other river

a lake where there was a road
where there was a lake

a growth from blood
& a directed line

in 1878 this address
was at the city limit

III.

three radiators in my apartment
some in a series, bled

in November for old warmth
heat rattle from lower floors

none above
the ceiling one thing, absolute

no where for heat to rise to
only slight cracks in window panes

cold air working in

floor boards burnt & warped
where fronts contact

some bits of plants fallen
from the windowsill

gathering at the roots
& dirt again

IV.

words & words & parts of words
& parts of others' words

an open window
sanctions the moving air

none of the doors in Frank St. seal their room
the common hall sounds clearly

where the weather proofing was torn out
the day we moved in

our neighbours' words
& the silence

V.

the wiring worries me
dad found its age

old enough to be dirt again if
it was bodies;

brief
a finger nail

but electric & stubborn

VI.

your fingers
& where they make familiar

& this room makes more sense

you arranged the furniture
while I picked up boxes

the things we carried here
& their shapes from light

our pillows match your birthmark

the ivy, & the umbrella, & the cactus
from Champagne

yes, we've kept these plants alive
& some days we remember

VII.

the front room closet door
does not shut

without an elbow

as though our coats & our recycling
& our tools

must be more accessible
than a doorknob

does the paint say so,
or the floorboards

making for the stairwell?

VIII.

my right hand dry
from washing the dishes

& your shoulders yielding

I still don't know what I'm doing
but I know doing it

sometimes I trace figures
into your muscles

poorly

I can't draw a circle & poem tries
I can draw a breath & poem tries

IX.

cold air in the hall
at the mailboxes

there is a crack, almost
a circle, in the window

the last breath of this &
a drop of fifty degrees

air best that sees our breathing

X.

we moved in September first
& I didn't notice the tree

outside the bedroom window
until spring & the snow

was under ground again

XI.

there is more furniture than
the day we moved in

yes, this room holds our books
& we hold each other

still, we fit today
& tomorrow

the things we carry
their accumulated shape

XII.

this morning, March fourth,
the sun rose

I marked your fingers, charged, first

tomorrow may wait under your hands
& this poorly made poem

I'm after your hands
all comes only

after your hands

XIII.

the sun, at
an ember pace

across the windows
at Metcalfe

& the copper edged roof
six houses down

in March I can't read
at five pm on the couch

the sun, & eyes
learn to stop

XIV.

see better, poem

see the shingles
lost this winter

see the old dust
at back of radiators

see where the floorboards give way
to footsteps, rehearsed

XV.

the south side snow
remains a while

after the north side
is clear

plants thrive
in the East window

I am trying to grow a beard

the ivy grows better

XVI.

old concrete stairs
to the alley

as wide as two feet

I see roots break
the sidewalk

none we make
holds still

XVII.

the smell of matches
on fingertips

more than the candle

steam from tea
on palms

your body gathering
where my fingers

reach

I am trying to write a poem

XVIII.

paint so heavy
you say it dulls the edges

cold water
before the shower goes hot

our neighbours doors opening
& it sounds like one house again

XIX.

feel the street sweeper
& the busses

over night

remember my fear
that the tall
bookcase won't

hold to the loose
dry wall

XX.

old books
& photocopies of older ones

the letters that
didn't transfer cleanly

newly empty spaces
in words

pinholes in the wall
where we move

photographs

XXI.

we walked home in the rain
& pressed it into our limbs

against windowpanes
over the bed & radiator

we're water at our best

bent before overflowing
more than lips should allow

water

that knows the curve
of bodies

XXII.

when the umbrella,
wind-pulled, hit the sidewalk

three floors down
the planter cracked

since, the roots have grown
in tight circles

around one another
                              outside the dirt

two years later
we have to cut the pot away

before replanting it

somewhere new
& large enough again

A HISTORY OF BUTTON COLLECTING

Helen Hajnoczky

A history of button collecting, of corrugated cardboard living. Scalloped edged photographs in newspaper lined drawers. Old birthday cards from aunts who remain steadfastly proud. One hundred in each grandparent card, then singular grandparent, then no more cards. A stuffed toy the pudgy hand of memory clings to, Muttsy, my plush puppy still fluffy, not matted from years of soothing me through nightmares. Night opens to lamplight where nightlights once peeked through the open door to crack the abyss of the floor harbouring a slithering nothing ready to brush against my feet if I get up to go to the bathroom. Only the yellow light, warm pouring in, to stain the walls with my mother's lullaby that I will be watched by angels, to purify the room and burn the terror from the walls.

❋

When now sepia not faded, ruby against a stone glare that broke the daylight. The evening, holding against a memory like your grey suits, trim beard, this first step towards a glide, your smell, not apparent but then apparently illuminating the winter gloom. I wouldn't notice each winter whittled you into a memory, and watered me into an old shelf full of photo albums. I grew out of the ground around you—you remain a seed of memory, hibernating in the frost.

Against the garden's gravity, tulips preen only gilded sunset stutters against tomorrow's dew, shadows each bead a length and then no watermark to hold up the sun. In the window, in the vase, a rose— baby's breath, still crisp and still. I cut this memory at an angle, put it in water. The vines twine around my heart. I hang the wilted moments from the ceiling; their graying shadows gather dust.

How holding could hold him like a moment had stole him to hold this position and wait for a storm that he hadn't imagined, and then something happened and a thick wet snow piled up around the house for days, every trip soaking my boots.

Bronze paisley, this damp upholstered memory of visiting your new basement apartment, and you hoard a chunk of this to live on every day, it sits and mildews in my mind, along with the time when I saw you every day. No copper plate covers these days, bronzed by the first stain of sunlight pouring into the classroom against the French grammar frozen stiff in the weak grip of this poem. Objects record these interactions—notebooks of pre-yellowed paper, unused pages—the book, a relic in its emptiness, a memory in its void.

❊

Swore office, no elevator, clipped walls and a corner window. Tar fire on Tuesday, then the bar. No corridor. Swore office and clotting. No corner to clip to. Fire of walls and windows. A corridor and then the bar. Clotting.

Blue stretched like sky across the ground, and ripples to rain, but crack cane of a lathe, struck sin on the roof, suck pain yet the sun blinks through. Like the tongue cradles each vowel—a seed for safekeeping. Poured over the back of each heavy summer day, or each aimless park visit, this chill and I cannot thaw your feet, cannot keep dowsing you with cold water, hoping you will breath, and the sunset—above abounds beyond, and I shelter myself in my skull—watch memories of skyscrapers open and welcome home my friends, brave enough to move on.

✵

Pastel smudge of sunset, cold memories cling like dust, crackle of gravel, the lane sheltered by an awning of oak trees. Press on and watch the sun go down. Cold gravel of memories, crackle of sunset like dust. Go down the lane, sheltered by an awning of sunset, oak trees watch the sun go down. Press on, a pastel smudge.

Night the coast, empty tiled walkway at a stretch. The sea breeze belies the moon's gaze, enrobes the breakers in a honeyed embrace. No cold crash of waves, moon rays burn away the roaring sigh. Empty walkway. Night's weight pressed upon the coast, tiled street to the palm caught on the edge of the beach, the edge of the ragged pull of the black ocean, its laboured gasps, hiss of the waves keep us balanced in the sand, against the crushing pull of emptiness.

❋

The waves sucked back to the sea where they break their own fall to pull themselves back and splash through the surf, the hiss of the waves, this splash of the day on the hills that break the caress of the sun on the back of the land and the palms that twist in the wind that flits through my hair and breathes through your hand when you take mine like the sand that sifts through my hand when I try to catch my breath.

Out of absence comes messes and out of staleness comes vapid assembling. Out of zippers comes ownership, and out of retrieval comes more laundry. So then the unpacking—is that a black way of being full, is something suggesting a home, and is it fully satisfying? It is not. It is so temporal to be frozen and see a solid substance permanently. It is so silly to expect an unpacking but not a packing again.

❋

Groan of old photographs, antique architecture—a cobblestone skyscraper stuck on the horizon, draped in the coal cradle of sunset—a bundle of breeze. Gold coal frozen against another silver hour, a diamond of light flickering past this life, a ruby sun, an emerald sea, the moment set in stone. Of course, time courses by. The clatter of evening—raw throat, grey blue. Sky at the end of a window, a tunnel of gazing, no failing to clap on my tongue. Reflection of walls in the polished floorboards of memory. Daybreak—the groan of morning splinters the curtains, warm shards dapple the bed. This day comes to rest—honeyed laudanum. I wake, and gather my regrets.

FOR WHEN YOU PICK DAISIES

Marilyn Irwin

road o dendro

as
toxic
gate

pretty
still

drawn
soft

sacred
shade

verbenabose

there it went
a part;
cookie,
penny spit spent

lullaby
verbenabose:

hat'll do
that'll do

spring sun
fruit skin
spidered web
nothing

what stemmed there

catatonic mulch chips
pebble shift
beetle forage

grass sway
all that
flutters by

green saplings
greedy brown

lineage of root
extending circumstance

untitled

bullfrog chorus kuhcoffaknee
until
their cattail cloak
starry toed croak
until
she, what then:
do they keep on
with their cyclical song
and
do they hear
the grass blades blow?

for when you pick daisies

I

for when you pick daisies:
sometimes, it's worth
not

don't pull the petals off;
knowing
at the same time

II

i have captured
your silver puddles
in christmas crackers
for when you plant
daisies in mine

would kiss
if only
within reach

your suffered speech
concrete caged coaxed

let me be
the ____
once

III
i stashed your silver puddles
in christmas crackers
for when you snap pull
into mine;

pricked the tip of my nose   know the smell of your thorns

you plant glass grass   closer to clover
sew sunshine secret   into meadow shadows
weave waves   watch sea strands saturate

non sequitur

kaleidoscope
confused with
mellow canopy
Dali dally

of

stick-tailed
birds perched
on dripping elm trees
in the heat haze

of

our space-age glow
our sunset slow
our tender
dark
pure

stain

porous regret
though I've none
my skin
bleach clean

except for
somewhere
i could never see

the droplets
of coffee
stain
on my coffee
table

no match
for the irony
of this metaphor

nocturne

fourfiftyone

cigarettesmoking

kindlescratch
forest fires

spark stars scream

lavamusic
tonight

forgotten (for Nick Drake)

road, less taken
fix to next
age-less-time

reverie recoil
painted coat cold
velvet tea
five leaves left

when will the needle trip
cough the fog
from your cereal bowl?

lullaby Jane
to sleep
from sleep
where sleep
stays dilated

to hit
another wall
before the river boat man;
your change

dystopic utopic sub-tropic of cancer

the susurrus of seasons
blown by
a dead ringing
in metropolitan ears

a dragon is caught in the atmosphere

black clouds
linger low
devour linings
consume temples

cracked sidewalks
heave paths
to away

poppy seeds

fermented step beyond

periodically

carving holes
in bagels
preserving poppy seeds
for a bagel tree
in a rusty mason jar

humidex

i am drunk off
your scent steam
lingers

august mist
bee sting
bug itch

sparks stream from cigarettes
casualties of war
fuse into fire escape

shift of sand sift

feather breath
kiss whispers
expose

soap scum scars
freckles there
that curve like pisces

the dirt on my window

is measured by the
frequency of neighbouring
cats and a desire to
leave your imaginary
fingerprints, carnation imprints
on the outside
feigning in

lessnowmore

purring
into pores
as you became
less white

I stole your
glasses
from the cat;

finally fallen
rabbit hole

what was said

tone of time
fine tuned
wax carvings
with our names
and the letters
never spoke
and the books
we didn't read
by ikea lamplight
safe
safe
sound

partly there

the sun
will probably
and set

indifferent

caterpillars

won't finish
will begin

i'm wearing

the same smile

IMPOSSIBLE BOOKS (THE CARLETON INSTALLMENT)

Stephen Brockwell

From the *Prime Minister's Nursery Rhymes for Insolent Children*

Animal Crackers

Crocodiles grind wildebeests.
Chickadees peep.
Starved lion prides kill elephants.
Koala bears sleep.

Hawks dig their talons one in inch deep.
Prairie dogs dig.
Timber wolves gnaw caribou.
Snorts the wild pig.

Sharks shred seal pups near the shore.
Hungry kittens cry.
Rock pythons crush small gazelles.
Little brown bats fly.

Shrikes impale mice on barbed wire.
Weaning calves keen.
Wild male chimps murder babies.
Silverbacks preen.

Tank commanders shell their friends.
Celebrities play.
Well dressed men sell cluster bombs.
Private school boys pray.

From the *Prime Minister's Nursery Rhymes for Insolent Children*

Jesus lives my little sheep.
Liberal members crawl and creep.

A country of this vast size
Must be ruled by one who is wise.

You must never apologize
For loving your strong leader.

Hush little ones, hush.
Shut your eyes.

From the *Evangelical Handbook for Engineers*

Fourier transforms will not detect
the chaotic music of the sinner's heart.
No load calculation will brace the atheist
against the weight of God's Word.
Six-sigma quality control will never eradicate
the defects of the wicked.
But if one Christian
enters your building,
drives across your bridge,
or operates your machinery,
let God inform each design and calculation.

From *The Love Poems of ______, Serial Killer*

They will tell you
a man who can kill cats
and women with surgical
precision is incapable of love.
A lie. I loved,
what was her name,
Anne. I loved her.
It is after all a word,
the tongue on the teeth,
the open mouth,
the teeth biting the lips
until they bleed.
I loved Anne.

From *The Archives of Ministry of Spiritual Ascendance, Folio 1027-3F, December 12, 2024*

Dear Ministry of Spiritual Ascendance,
I believe I should be accepted for God
because I have never eaten meat.
I cultivated tomatoes at my window
from a pack of ancient seeds.
I nurtured them to the size
of vitamins with water I filtered
from the rain. That Saturday morning
I prayed for the Sun as I am sure
so many do every day but I prayed
for others not for myself
and the Sun appeared for at least
one minute through the smog.
All my life I have shared the gifts I have received.
But I am so tired – please accept this
application for God.

From *The Archives of Ministry of Spiritual Ascendance*, **Folio 924-7B, July 20, 2023**

Dear Ministry of Spiritual Ascendance,
I no longer perform work of value.
I spend my day scavenging dumpsters
or stewing mice waiting for my end.
I use few resources – a little water
to wash, to brew tea and to cook.
A little gas for heat on the coldest days.
But could not this, even this, give hope
to one young mother and her child?
I truly am an unselfish man.
There is no reason why you should not
accept my application for God.
Surely the Ministry cannot be so cruel
as to force a broken old man to go on living.

from *Pindaric Odes to the Objects of Science*, **by Wilhelm Scheif**

Best of all things has always been you, water,
        trillions of your tilted flying Vs in
                each human, fish and worm, each suck or sip
of breast milk, juice, ale, wine, tea and morphine,
        each pre- and post- coital fluid (spit, sweat, tears
                et cetera – to the uncertain greeting
        of the egg and seed).

At least one molecule of you in me
        passed through the body of some great person,
                in the urine of Josef Stalin, say,
on an October morning in his youth;
        it may be one I am passing on now
                as a drop of saliva flies from my tongue
        over this paper.

Better yet, one of your numberless flowed
        through the Norman tongue of Pierre Trudeau
                paddling down the Lievre in buckskin
or trudging through a blizzard on the Hill.
        May that one lodge in a dormant neuron
                of an untapped cortex of my brain,
        singing of glaciers.

From *Metonymies: Poems by Objects Owned by Illustrious People*

Stephen Harper's Shoes

Long days holding up the country,
short nights breathing fresh air.
Each morning, a minion polishes away
a day's accumulated scuffs
with matt black petroleum paste.
My burnished upper reflects the blurred image
of the face above but does not shine.
My heel grinds even the iridescent
beetle, silent, powerless, beautiful,
Into the Langevin asphalt. My steel
shank would never pass security
if the face did not control it personally.
The feet have no particular smell,
like winter air or snow. I complain
of the unguents, salves and balms, reeking of sulphur
that, despite all evidence to the contrary, will not
relieve the cracked and callused heels.

From *Sonnets for Business* **by John McCairn, Vice President of Operations, CanSpo**

Parrots not in Cleveland

Parrots were celebrities in Panama.
March snow in Cleveland diminishes
not one feather of their famous cackles,

imitating Jim Cagney's "Dirty rat!"
while chattering patrons sipped banana
daiquiris from tumblers topped with parasols

to keep the infamous parrot guano
from fouling up their rum. I can imitate
a parrot's colour and voice. I'll need a trumpet,

a trunk full of Hawaiian shirts, a pair
of holey sneakers spattered with blue paint,
a month of sunlight to give this snow the shaft,

sandpaper to smooth my shovel calluses,
your naked throat to tune my parrot tongue.

Hemmingway's Bistro, Oak Park, Illinois

Maples in Oak Park Illinois: their keys spin
like the finger of a girl obsessively twirling a strand
of brown hair while reading a hardbound book
or watching cartoons on the tube.

Wisconsin venison tastes as good as it sounds:
fattened with grain, it lacks that gamey tang
but butters the teeth with blood, pepper and marsala wine.
If this country stopped coddling its youth like meat

how happy the world would be: the lovely
babies laughing in Kirkuk, the Roma
dancing in Prague, the Innu throat-singing
in Madison, the Sunni spinning in Trieste.

Garcon, Peter, you fled Krakov for Chicago.
What broken man or woman did you abandon via Paris
for this Nation of occasional courtesy, fine wines,
V8 boneyards and ambitious health insurance saleswomen?

FURTHER TO OUR CONVERSATION

Robert Kroetsch

Dear John Lent,

We wash ashore from our mothers wearing nothing but a few hairs. Our first cry is a poem that contains everything.

Strictly speaking, peanuts are not nuts. It was a wet night, so you rowed home. I suppose you could claim we have learned to walk without legs. That would be the short answer. Never mention the moon in a poem, that's what I always say.

Cantilevers can cross a chasm from cliff to cliff. The converse is also correct. The Beowulf poet was onto something. Figs and apricots, set in the sun, could be said to be soaking in sunlight. Given that, then, the thought becomes a thong.

On bad days we are little more than road kill.

You were riding shotgun on your motor home when the thunder rolled. Coconut cream pie is just about the best thing going. If I had my way, giraffes would have shorter necks and longer legs, errant snakes would be hanged by the neck, Dewey Decimal would organize our highways once and for all.

You knelt too close to the fire. You might be a ruse, a reconnoitering. Icarus in a car, disguise the limits, pain.

Capitalists and other high rollers wear expensive shoes. Certainties are short-lived, and fallacies are, by and large, true, or somewhat true, or briefly true, or not untrue, with exceptions as noted. Poets might not have wings, but they have toenails. Your poems are catapults. Please unfasten your seat belts now.

A licence plate has an odd destiny. It is not allowed to make words out of the ABCs.

You May Not Know the Sender

This message is from you.
It says: Please do not open.

Dear Nicole Markotić,

Saw you there on that rainbow. Be careful. But not too careful. Rainbows make quite a racket.

I would prefer you didn't use the word you didn't use. Coyotes are bad enough to begin with, mouths open, luring the sun. The yellow pages, a difficult narrative, the absurdity of order. Make mine one egg, over easy.

My silence is only the silence of silence. Tomatoes are a different matter, and poisonous mushrooms, not to mention dump trucks. Jazz gives guidance to flocks of geese. Pelicans, on the other hand, glide close to the waves.

Your home takes you everywhere. Everybody we know is busy dying. Your feet want to go dancing. Even if asphodels were prairie flowers we would hesitate at the gates of the underworld, nor would we, at least very often, try to explain, flowers being as they are, what we call flowers, time being its own version of logic. For the time, being. If in doubt, consult the yellow pages. We drowse at the edge of reason.

Perhaps a flower is a prism. It turns light into rainbows.

Perhaps there is no present, only the immediate future and the immediate past. Consider the experience of finding a nest of dinosaur eggs in a Red Deer River coulee. We might as well write poems.

We Will Never be Lovers if You Keep This Up

You pushed the ladder away
when I tried to climb in your window.
It was black as love outside.

You could have had a bad fall.
I wouldn't want that to happen.
Next time I'll warn you in advance.

Dear Jeff Carpenter,

A fog of understanding engulfed the whirled. We lubricate the axle with our tears. St Teresa, please, hand me a Kleenex. Don't fall out of bed.

It must be the large intestine. What else would play Snakes and Ladders? Accidents are, possibly, more mobile and connotative.

I'm trying to find a use for the word, kinetic. Stasis is food for cats. Punctuation is a middle-class pretension. So is a toothache. In heaven you have to sit eternally staring at a bright light, so be sure to take your dark glasses.

I heard a shadow. Who else would eat raw garlic on a slab of black bread? Your new Manifesto, like Heaven, like Love, can only exist if it does not exist.

Carbuncle tends towards two meanings. But then, who doesn't? Earlier in the year we wintered in the tropics, only to discover that, given what we know, given what it cost us, parrots are not to be trusted, and, even if they were, we wouldn't.

We lounge toward the infinite. Death, that necessary pest.

I once travelled halfway across Spain to see St Teresa's bent left elbow safe in a glass jar. We each write the poem as we see fit. But then, what poem isn't a relic?

After Sleep

the woman he dreamed he loved ...
was not the woman he loved ....
but was ... he slowly recognized ...

her immediate hair ...
the remoteness of her ankles ...
A hand of hers that was not asleep.

THE CREEKS:

rob mclennan

> Mercy does not come from the sky
> Norma Cole, *Coleman Hawkins Ornette Coleman*

Watershed. Stretched, a bend. Erupts. To be vulgar, coarse. Urban song, a thread of water. Spills. Underground, a Mohawk sky. We catch the rain. It snowflakes, tongue. Dark, manifold. So much a mirror, corner. Questions, held. Held up. This constellation, margin. Deeper than fulfilled, arthritic postures. We were not afraid. Thin, silent, mouths. Eye on you and then.

⋆

Search. We hold the river, down. This resolution, meets. Mouth to concentration, mouth. I can't go. No stream made, out-of-print. Useless, feathered, goods. What drawn and twisted, space. Snow warrant. Thin portraits. A simple-minded function. What ritual, thing. The trees, the skimming moon. Bookstalls. A brittle, darkened room. The pavement, ear. Abyss. Tonal waves direct.

⋆

Atlantic, between. Heavy manner, a centred abyss. This battered dawn, bashed ancient stone. The remains of civilization. First thought, Ur-thought. Grotesque. The ocean's subdivision. Tactless. Define a score, a roundabout, a hedge. A supernatural crescent. This heated, cooling effort. Passive, energized. History, become a mine. A gravel tendril. Soothe. You, who are large in our eyes.

AUTHOR BIOGRAPHIES

Cameron Anstee lives and writes in Ottawa ON where he runs Apt. 9 Press and is pursuing a PhD in English Literature at the University of Ottawa.

derek beaulieu is the author or editor of 15 books, the most recent of which are *Writing Surfaces: The Selected Fiction of John Riddell* (co-edited with Lori Emerson) and *Please, No more poetry: the poetry of derek beaulieu* (edited by Kit Dobson) both of which are published by Wilfrid Laurier University press. He is the publisher of the acclaimed no press and is the visual poetry editor at UBUWeb. He has contributed to fashion magazines such as *Flaunt*, *Hobo* and *The Block*, literary magazines such as *The Capilano Review* and *Poetry* and is a columnist at Lemonhound. beaulieu has exhibited his work across Canada, the United States and Europe and currently teaches at the Alberta College of Art + Design. In October 2013 he is starting his PhD at Roehampton University.

Gregory Betts is a poet, editor, scholar, and professor at Brock University in St. Catharines, Ontario. He is the author of five books of poetry, including *If Language* (BookThug 2005), *The Others Raisd in Me* (Pedlar Press 2009), and *The Obvious Flap* (with Gary Barwin BookThug 2011). His visual art collaborations with Matt Donovan, Hallie Siegel, and Neil Hennessy have been exhibited in numerous cities around Canada, including at the Olga Korper Gallery in Toronto, and are about to embark on a 7 year cross-continental tour. He is also the author of *Avant-Garde Canadian Literature: The Early Manifestations* (University of Toronto Press 2013) and his next book, *Boycott*, is forthcoming from Make Now Press.

Stephanie Bolster's latest book, *A Page from the Wonders of Life on Earth*, was shortlisted for the Pat Lowther Award, and an excerpt from her current project was chosen as a finalist for the CBC/Canada Writes competition in 2012. Her first book, *White Stone: The Alice Poems*, won the Governor General's Award and the Gerald Lampert Award in 1998; her first chapbook, *Three Bloody Words*, appeared with above/ground press in 1996. She edited *The Best Canadian Poetry in English 2008* and *The Ishtar Gate: Last and Selected Poems* by the Ottawa poet Diana Brebner, and co-edited *Penned: Zoo Poems*. Born in Vancouver, she teaches creative writing at Concordia University and lives in Pointe-Claire, Québec.

Stephen Brockwell is an Ottawa poet and entrepreneur. His book *Fruitfly Geographic* won the Archibald Lampman Award in 2005. Along with rob mclennan, Stephen was a featured reader at the Goldmine in New Orleans, Louisiana in May of 2012. *Improbable Books (the Carleton Installment)* is from *The Compete Surprising Fragments of Improbable Books* scheduled for publication by Mansfield Press, and is the second of three chapbooks by Stephen Brockwell produced through above/ground press.

Emily Carr directs the Low Residency MFA at Oregon State University Cascades. She is passionate about the rediscovery of Mississippi poet besmilr brigham, the sexual politics of meat, the limits of Achilles' honesty and the problem of Chaucer's spring, unposted love letters, cannibal chickens and a ship too late to save the drowning witch. Emily is the author of two books of poetry, *directions for flying* (Furniture Press 2010) and *13 Ways of Happily: Books 1 & 2* (Parlor Press 2011); a love trilogy of chapbooks, *Up The Shinbone Superlatives* (horseless press, 2012), *Resurrection Refrains* (dancing girl press, 2013), and *Stay This Moment: The Autopsy Lyrics Acts 1 & 2* (Little Red Leaves Textile Series, 2013); an epistolary erasure essay, *The Weights Of Heaven* (Western Humanities Review, 2011); and a Tarot novel.

Mark Cochrane lives in Vancouver, BC, practises law, and teaches in the English Department at Kwantlen Polytechnic University. He is the author of *Boy Am I* (Wolsak & Wynn), *Change Room* (Talonbooks), and, more recently, a chapbook called *Cat.* (above/ground press). His poetry, essays, or interviews with contemporary writers have appeared in journals including *New American Writing, The Capilano Review, Open Letter*, and *The Malahat Review*; textbooks (*Elements of English 11*); and anthologies (*A Verse Map of Vancouver, White Noise: The Eminem Collection*). He has written book reviews, encyclopedia entries, and materials relating to the practice of family law. He has a manuscript-in-progress called *Girlfriend of the Time.*

Amanda Earl is chuffed to have two broadsides and three chapbooks published by above/ground press and thanks shepherd rob mclennan for herding all of us troublesome lambs. Connect with Amanda on Twitter @KikiFolle or read all about her on amandaearl.com

Eric Folsom was recently short-listed for the long poem contest at *The Malahat Review*. He is the author of three books of poetry, he is presently the Poet Laureate of the City of Kingston in Ontario, and he once appeared on stage with Stuart MacLean's Vinyl Cafe, an event which also featured the remarkable and talented Sarah Harmer. But she probably doesn't remember. Why would she?

Born in 1947 in Brockville, Ontario. **Artie Gold** appeared like a supernova within the constellation of Montreal Anglophone poets in the late 1960s. Intensely devoted to poetry, having already discovered the work of Frank O'Hara, John Wieners and Jack Spicer in his teens, six books of his poems were published in each of the years 1974-79. Daunted by asthma, complicated by rapidly proliferating allergies and emphysema, he increasingly retreated from the world. At the urging of his friends, a selected poems, *The Beautiful Chemical Waltz* was published in 1992. His *The Collected Books of Artie Gold*, was published in 2010. Artie left the world on St. Valentine's Day, 2007. His nine published books shine like a beacon of Northern Lights across the literary landscape of the late twentieth century.

Helen Hajnoczky's first book *Poets and Killers: A Life in Advertising* was published in 2010 by Snare Books, an imprint of Invisible Publishing. She blogs http://ateacozyisasometimes.blogspot.ca/ and tweets @helenhajnoczky.

Sharon Harris is a Toronto writer/artist whose first book, *Avatar*, was published by The Mercury Press. Her work is forthcoming in *The Broadview Introduction to Literature*.

William Hawkins has lived most of his life in Ottawa, with side trips to Vancouver, Toronto, Tallahassee and Mexico. He is a veteran driver of the Blue Line taxi corps and includes prominent MPs, judges, journalists and bagmen among his regular clients. In recent years, Hawkins made a CD of his best songs, titled *Dancing Alone*, and was subject of an onstage tribute at the Ottawa Folk Festival for his contributions to the music scene. His collections of poetry include *Ottawa Poems* (Kitchener: weed/flower press, 1966), *The Gift of Space* (Toronto: New Press, 1971) and *Dancing Alone: Selected Poems* (Fredericton NB: Broken Jaw Press, 2005), with more recent chapbook publications through above/ground press and Apt. 9 Press. His online home is www.wmhawkins.com

The winner of *Arc Poetry Magazine*'s 2013 Diana Brebner Prize, **Marilyn Irwin**'s work has been published by above/ground press, *Bywords*, *ottawater*, The Peter F. Yacht Club, and most recently, the Canadian section of this year's *New American Writing*. A graduate of Algonquin College's Creative Writing program, she has released three chapbooks: *for when you pick daisies* (above/ground press, 2010), *flicker* (above/ground press, 2012), and *little nothings* (2012).

D.G. Jones was born in Ontario in 1929. He has won the Governor General's Award twice (for poetry in 1977 and for translation in 1993). His poetry has also won two QSPELL Awards and the A.J.M. Smith Award. Jones retired from teaching at the Université de Sherbrooke in 1994. He now lives in North Hatley, Quebec. *The Stream Exposed With All Its Stones: Collected Poems* came out with Vehicule Press in 2009.

Renowned poet, novelist, essayist and teacher, **Robert Kroetsch** (1927-2011) was one of Canada's most accomplished authors. With a career spanning well over 40 years, Kroetsch received numerous honours, including the prestigious Governor General's Literary Award for his book *The Studhorse Man*, and penned nine internationally acclaimed novels, fourteen books of poetry, and five books of non-fiction, essays, and exploration. Celebrated as a leading creator of contemporary Canadian literature, his writing, teaching, and critical vision helped shape Canadian literature and culture. His works have been translated, published, and studied extensively worldwide, and he gave readings in countries as various as China, Japan, Finland, Italy, and Australia. Kroetsch taught and mentored countless writers throughout the world. A Fellow of the Royal Society of Canada, he was short-listed for the Governor General's Literary Award in 2000 for *The Hornbooks of Rita K*. A Distinguished Alumnus of the University of Alberta, his most recent award was the Manitoba Arts Council Arts Award of Distinction.

Gil McElroy is a poet, independent curator, art critic, and visual artist. He has published four books of poetry, most recently *Ordinary Time* (Talonbooks, 2011), and numerous chapbooks that include *Ordinary Time: The Merton Lake Propers* (Baseline Press, 2012). He is also author of *Gravity & Grace: Selected Writing on Contemporary Canadian Art* (Gaspereau Press, 2001) and the memoir *Cold Comfort: Growing Up Cold War* (Talonbooks, 2012). McElroy writes about visual art for publications in Canada and the United States, and is a regular correspondent for Akimblog. As a practicing visual artist, he has recently been collaborating with Halifax-based artist Peter Dykhuis on a series of site-specific gallery exhibitions based on abandoned Cold War military installations in Canada. His fourth above/ground press chapbook, *Twentieth*, appeared in February, 2013. He lives in the village of Colborne, Ontario with his wife Heather.

Born in Ottawa, Canada's glorious capital city, **rob mclennan** currently lives in Ottawa. The author of more than twenty trade books of poetry, fiction and non-fiction, he won the John Newlove Poetry Award in 2011, and was longlisted for the CBC Poetry Prize in 2012. His most recent titles are the poetry collections *Songs for little sleep*, (Obvious Epiphanies, 2012) and a second novel, *missing persons* (2009). *The Uncertainty Principle: stories*, is forthcoming with Chaudiere Books, as is a collection of essays, *Notes and Dispatches*, from Insomniac Press. An editor and publisher, he runs above/ground press, Chaudiere Books, *The Garneau Review*, *seventeen seconds: a journal of poetry and poetics* and the Ottawa poetry pdf annual *ottawater*. He spent the 2007–8 academic year in Edmonton as writer-in-residence at the University of Alberta, and regularly posts reviews, essays, interviews and other notices at robmclennan.blogspot.com

Nathanaël (formerly Nathalie Stephens) is the author of a score of books written in English or French, most recently, *Sisyphus, Outdone. Theatres of the Catastrophal* (2012), *Carnet de somme* (2012), and *We Press Ourselves Plainly* (2010). *Je Nathanaël* (2003) exists in self-translation (2006) as does the essay of correspondence, *Absence Where As (Claude Cahun and the Unopened Book)* (2009), first published in French as *L'absence au lieu* (2007). Nathanaël's extrinsic translations include works by Hervé Guibert, Danielle Collobert, Édouard Glissant, Catherine Mavrikakis, and Hilda Hilst, the latter in collaboration with Rachel Gontijo Araújo. She lives in Chicago.

Monty Reid is an Ottawa writer. His most recent books are *Disappointment Island* (Chaudiere) and *The Luskville Reductions* (Brick). He monitors Canada's spy agencies.

Lisa Samuels has published seven poetry books, recently *Gender City* (2011) and *Wild Dialectics* (2012). She is also the author of four chapbooks, a 2-CD poetry work with soundscapes, essays and edited work in poetry, cultural theory, and critical practice, and a creative non-fiction book, *Anti M* (2013). Born in Boston, she has lived in North America, Europe, the Middle East, and Australasia. Since 2006 she has taught literature, theory, and creative writing in Aotearoa / New Zealand.

Natalie Simpson's *accrete or crumble*, was published by LINEbooks in 2006. Her poetry has appeared in *Shift & Switch: New Canadian Poetry* (Mercury), *Post-Prairie: An Anthology of New Poetry* (Talonbooks), and *Shy: An Anthology* (University of Alberta Press). Talonbooks will publish her next book of poetry, *Thrum*, in early 2014. She practices pro bono law in Calgary, Alberta and curates *filling Station magazine*'s flywheel Reading Series.

Aaron Tucker's poetic works and reviews have been published across Canada. His chapbook, *apartments*, was shortlisted for the 2010 bpNichol Chapbook award; he also published chapbook versions of *apartments*, *section three* and *punchlines 1.0* with above/ground press. His collection of essays *Interfacing with the Internet in Popular Cinema* is going to be published by Palgrave-Macmillan in the summer of 2014. In addition, he is a professor in the English department at Ryerson University where he is currently teaching essay writing and digital literacy to first year students. He is working on learning chess in between watching his beloved Raptors lose games.

Julia Williams is a poet, prose writer and copywriter who lives in Calgary with an Englishman and some kids. Her first book of poetry, *The Sink House*, was published by Coach House Books in 2004.

Suzanne Zelazo is a writer, editor and elite triathlete.

Rachel Zolf's writing practice explores interrelated materialist questions concerning memory, history, knowledge, subjectivity, and the conceptual limits of language and meaning. She is particularly interested in how ethics founders on the shoals of the political. She has four books of poetry, with proverbial awards and nominations, under her proverbial belt. A film she wrote for New York artist Josiah McElheny about queers bathing in light premiered at Art Basel Miami Beach 2012. Her fifth book, *Janey's Arcadia*, is forthcoming with Coach House in Fall 2014. The juvenilia excerpt published here, "the naked & the nude," was a homage to Phyllis Webb, John Berger, Betsy Warland, Audre Lorde, Joni Mitchell, and Bob Marley.

ACKNOWLEDGMENTS

Artie Gold, “doublet” originally appeared in an edition of approximately 30 copies and printed by Artie Gold through Barry McKinnon’s Caledonia Writing Series, Prince George, B.C. in the spring of 1978. It later appeared as above/ground press broadside #157, October 2002, and is reprinted here with the kind permission of the Literary Estate of Artie Gold.

Mark Cochrane. “Rotator Cuff at 33 1/3” above/ground press broadsheet #167, March 2003.

Suzanne Zelazo. “SUIT” above/ground press broadside #170. April 2003.

Stephanie Bolster. “Night Zoo” appeared as above/ground press broadside #289, March 2009.

Amanda Earl. “ivre” appeared as above/ground press broadside #260, April 2007.

Nathanaël. “what exile   this” STANZAS *magazine*, issue #29, February 2002.

Lisa Samuels. “The Museum of Perception” STANZAS *magazine*, issue #33, October 2002.

Rachel Zolf. “the naked & the nude” STANZAS *magazine*, issue #40, June 2004.

Sharon Harris. “more fun with ‘pataphysics” STANZAS *magazine*, issue #41, January 2006.

D.G. Jones. *standard pose*. February 2002.

Julia Williams. *My City Is Ancient And Famous*. August 2004.

Eric Folsom. *Northeast Anti-ghazals*, January 2005. A second printing appeared in September 2011.

Gregory Betts. *The Cult of David Thompson*, January 2005.

Natalie Simpson. “Writing the writing,” originally appeared as the chapbook *The writing that should enter into conversation*, April 2005.

Monty Reid. *cuba A book*. June 2005.

William Hawkins. *The black prince of bank street*. August 2007.

Emily Carr. *& look there goes a sparrow transplanting soil*. December 2009.

Aaron Tucker. *apartments, section three*. March 2010.

Cameron Anstee. *Frank St*. March 2010.

Helen Hajnoczky. *A history of button collecting*. March 2010.

Marilyn Irwin. *for when you pick daisies*. July 2010.

Stephen Brockwell. *Impossible Books (the Carleton Installment)*. August 2010.

Robert Kroetsch. *Further to Our Conversation*. July 2011. It is reprinted here with the kind permission of the Literary Estate of Robert Kroetsch.

rob mclennan, "The creeks" appeared in the chapbook *The creeks*, July 2013.

COLOPHON

Typeset in Quadraat and Quadraat Sans by Christine McNair in Adobe InDesign and printed at Marquis Printing.

Quadraat was designed by Fred Smeijers, author of *Counterpunch* in 1996. FF Quadraat Sans was described by Smeijers as "not just humanist but very humanist, and quite a character among the sanses." Quadraat Sans is narrow and a little spiky; in a block of text, it has more variance in colour than most sans serifs.

OTHER CHAUDIERE BOOKS TITLES

Casemate Poems (Collected), Joe Blades. 2011, poetry, 978-0-9783428-1-4

The Lizard and Other Stories, Michael Bryson. 2010, short stories, 978-0-9783428-3-8

been shed bore, Pearl Pirie. 2010, poetry, 978-0-9783428-5-2

Soft where, Marcus McCann. 2009, poetry, 978-0-9783428-4-5

A Long Continual Argument: The Selected Poems of John Newlove. Edited by Robert McTavish with afterword by Jeff Derksen. 2007, poetry, 978-0-9781601-1-1

Old Winter, Anne Le Dressay. 2007, poetry, 978-0-9783428-0-7

The Ottawa City Project, rob mclennan. 2007, poetry, 978-0-9781601-6-6

Decalogue 2 : ten Ottawa fiction writers. Edited by rob mclennan. 2007, fiction, 978-0-9781601-4-2

Everything is Movies, Nicholas Lea. 2007, poetry, 978-0-9781601-7-3

The Desmond Road Book of the Dead, Clare Latremouille. 2006, fiction, 978-0-9781601-2-8

Disappointment Island, Monty Reid. 2006, poetry, 978-0-9781601-1-1

movements in jars, Meghan Jackson. 2006, poetry, 978-0-9781601-0-4

Decalogue: ten Ottawa poets. Edited by rob mclennan. 2006, poetry, 978-0-9781601-3-5

Ground rules : the best of the second decade of above/ground press 2003-2013 / edited by rob mclennan ; with an introduction by Gil McElroy.

ISBN 978-0-9783428-7-6 (pbk.)

1. Canadian poetry (English)--21st century. 2. Canadian poetry (English)--20th century. I. McLennan, Rob, 1970-, editor of compilation

PS8293.1.G76 2013 C811'.5408 C2013-907388-4

WWW.CHAUDIEREBOOKS.COM